IDAHO'S WILDERNESS VISIONARY:

HARRY SHELLWORTH

RICHARD H. HOLM, JR.

[signature]

COLD MOUNTAIN PRESS

D1616127

Other titles by R.H. Holm, Jr.:
Points of Prominence: Fire Lookouts of the Payette National Forest
Bound for the Backcountry: A History of Idaho's Remote Airstrips
Bound for the Backcountry II: A History of Airstrips in the Wallowas, Hells Canyon, and the Lower Salmon River

To purchase copies of *Idaho's Wilderness Visionary: Harry Shellworth* contact author at boundforthebackcounty@gmail.com

Published by Cold Mountain Press, McCall, ID

Cover photograph: Harry Shellworth, 1933 enjoying the wilds of Idaho. Photograph by Johnson & Son and courtesy of the Shellworth Family Collection.

Cover and interior design by TeaBerryCreative.com

ISBN: 978-0-578-85609-4

First Edition

Printed in the United States of America

For the Harry Shellworth Family

TABLE OF CONTENTS

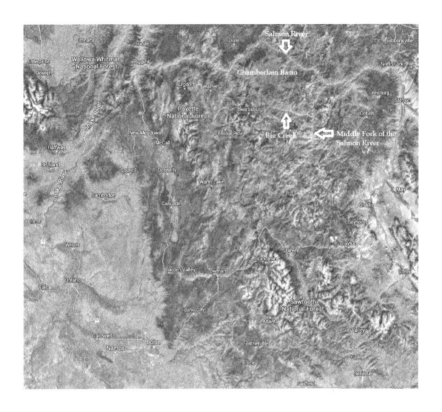

SOUTH-CENTRAL IDAHO POINTS OF INTEREST. *(Google Earth 2021)*

MCCALL AREA POINTS OF INTEREST. (*Google Earth 2021*)

FOREWORD

"Pay no attention to that man behind the curtain," the Wizard of Oz instructed Dorothy. Of course, that's exactly what we care about, the one behind the curtain, the one pulling the levers, coming up with the ideas, introducing people to each other, putting in the effort to make good things happen here in Idaho.

For my money, author Richard H. Holm, Jr. has found that person and introduced him to us in this publication. And the best thing about it...Harry Shellworth is everything we'd want him to be. Not full of himself, but down to earth; someone comfortable hobnobbing with senators and governors, as well as hermits on the banks of the remote Salmon River.

As host and producer of Idaho Public Television's *Outdoor Idaho* series for more than thirty years, how I wish we could have interviewed Harry for our show! But he died in 1973 at the age of ninety-six.

We do have the next best thing, however: this book by master investigator Holm, who received an Esto Perpetua Award from the Idaho State Historical Society in 2015 for his preservation efforts. Others had thought of writing a biography of the man referred to in an *Idaho Statesman* essay as "The Most Unforgettable Man I Ever Met."

But it was Richard, who—approached by the Shellworth family—actually pulled it off, spending years poring over Harry's copious notes, tracking as best he could the man's many adventures.

I first came upon Harry Shellworth's handiwork when my buddies and I began exploring one of Idaho's "primitive areas" in the 1960s. Only later did I learn the rest of the story. Shellworth would make annual trips into the Salmon River Mountains, along Big Creek, a tributary of the Middle Fork of the Salmon River. And he loved to invite friends to join him for these extended trips.

One trip in particular stood out. In 1927 he gathered together a Forest Service official, a mining executive, a lawyer, a photographer, a forester, and Idaho Governor H. Clarence Baldridge. Harry was concerned that civilization was encroaching upon his favorite part of the state.

You can imagine the spirited conversations around the campfire night after night, as they hashed out the notion of an "Idaho Primitive Area" encompassing the vast expanse of land between the Middle Fork, the South Fork, and the main Salmon River.

It was an audacious idea; but, in the fullness of time, it led to the nation's largest forested wilderness, the Frank Church River of No Return Wilderness Area.

Holm tells that story in what is my favorite chapter of the book. Other chapters deal with Harry's involvement with the Civilian Conservation Corps, Idaho's forest fire lookouts, tourism in the

McCall area, and the science of timber management. Harry was employed by the Boise Payette Lumber Company, where he helped create the Southern Idaho Timber Protective Association.

A personal observation here: This gregarious, down-to-earth man was a proud member of the mainstream Republican Party, a strong believer in private property and state's rights. And yet, when Harry's special part of Idaho was threatened, he quickly turned to the federal government for help. It was a strategy later used by US Senator Frank Church in sponsoring the Wilderness Act of 1964 and the 1968 Wild and Scenic Rivers Act. That's because it often takes local, state, and federal cooperation to get big things accomplished.

Harry never ran for political office. Yet William Borah called him "Idaho's politician anonymous," a fitting description of a man who preferred to work behind the scenes. As Harry saw it, "politics is simply the science of harmonizing the interests of the most people… whatever they may be, sons-of-bitches or priests."

Today hardly anyone knows his name.

But that might change with the publication of this book. And for that we owe Richard a debt of gratitude. He did the heavy lifting to bring Harry Shellworth out of the shadows for a new generation to appreciate…Idaho's man behind the curtain.

BRUCE REICHERT
Outdoor Idaho, Idaho Public Television

1

THE EARLY YEARS AND SETTLING DOWN

She [Boise] sits embowered in deep shade, one of the pleasantest
of towns, in a valley as fruitful and flowery as the valley of the
Po or the Rhone. Yet most of the valley is reclaimed land, on the
edge of the desert. Boise is in a sense an outpost, a fortress.
—ANNE O'HARE MCCORMICK
An American Epic in Sand and Flame (1931)

Who was Harry Shellworth? Not many Idahoans other than a few historians can answer this question today. If the same question were posed a hundred or even fifty years ago, residents state-wide would have described the man most knew, or at least knew of, simply as Harry. For Harry Shellworth wore many hats, personally and publicly, some of which could be perceived as contradictory, as he could be identified as a lumberman one minute and a preservationist

1

the next. Between the two extremes Harry might modestly be tagged as a proud veteran, an outdoorsman, statesman, politician, lobbyist, conservationist, or a family man. Notable achievements include the creation of the Southern Idaho Timber Protective Association (SITPA), the establishment of the Civilian Conservation Corps (CCC) in the state of Idaho, and most remarkable of all—the establishment of the Idaho Primitive Area, now the heart of the Frank Church River of No Return Wilderness—the second largest federally designated wilderness area in the lower forty-eight states. Paying tribute to his work during his lifetime, three landmarks in Valley County were named in his honor—an island on Payette Lake, a spring along Red Ridge, and a beach in McCall. While Harry Shellworth is no longer a household name as it was in the Progressive or New Deal eras of Idaho and the American West, the efforts of his life work can be observed widely today throughout the state.

Harry was born to Julian and Mary Luticia (Campbell) Shellworth on May 20, 1877, the first of seven children who resided on a ranch in Comanche, Texas. His father, thirty-two at the time, was not only a rancher but also a lawman. The German-born Julian had moved his family to the Lone Star State from Brooklyn, New York, where he previously spent less than a year in the military (enlisted February 1867). From Texas Julian moved his family to Walla Walla, Washington, for one year and then to Boise in October 1890, just four months after Idaho became a state, where he took a job as a police captain and also ran a horse livery business. In the bustling city of Boise (population 2,500), Harry, age thirteen, found a job working as a newspaper boy for *The Idaho Daily Statesman* and as a telegraph messenger. He also worked as a page during the first session of the Idaho legislature. Describing the experience years later, Harry commented, "[I] got to know the big men from all over the State and the fascination of having them talk to me as if I was one of them had me hypnotized... was like Bourbon to my ego."[1] Harry was destined to be in politics.

Harry never let the grass grow under his feet and he left Idaho before graduating from Boise High School. While he yearned for adventure, the primary catalyst for leaving home was pressure from his mother to become a First Presbyterian minister—something for which Harry had no desire. For the next eleven years he traveled the world.[2] This wanderlust transformed him into the larger-than-life character he became as an adult. Harry was a known storyteller—and a very good one. For the rest of his life he drew upon these vagabond years for his campfire tales and they were captivating.

In brief, when he first left Boise he headed to San Francisco where he finagled his way into a job as a cabin boy on a passenger ship, the *S.S. Santa Ana*, on a trip to Panama. He then returned to Boise. His mother again insisted that he become a minister, "[S]o I beat it again." This time he headed to Portland, Oregon, and worked for Wadhams & Kerr Wholesale Grocery Company, which he decried as "lame." He then buddied-up with a young law student and drifted to Alaska where they joined the Klondike Gold Rush. The gold rush adventure ended poorly in May 1897 on the Dyea Trail, "[W]here we were blackjacked on the trail, out of Summit City, and robbed...they even took the mackinaw coats off our backs. Summit City's citizens took up a fund to help us back to Skagway where I saw the cadaver of one of the thugs." Harry, thinking he was ready to settle down, returned

---

1   Harry C. Shellworth. *Travel-Log North Pacific Ocean (1893-1904)*. March 1970, 1. Shellworth Family Collection.

2   Shellworth. *Travel-Log North Pacific Ocean (1893-1904)*. 1.

to Portland and life with the grocery company. However, again the "lame" life was not for Harry, and within a year he joined the Idaho First Volunteers, which dispatched him on assignments with the US Army on transport ships where he bounced around the globe finding himself somehow involved with major world events such as the Nome Gold Rush (Alaska), the Boxer Rebellion, the Spanish-American War, and the Philippine-American War.[3] One of the closer brushes with death for Harry came during the Philippine-American War at the Battle of Manila (also known as the Battle of Santa Ana). The gruesome two-day battle between February 4 and 5, 1899, ended with an American victory and Harry being hit with a tiny piece of bomb shrapnel in his right ear lobe. Making light of the injury Harry said, "[It] entitled me [to] extra pension—$14.50 per month for 'wounded in action.'"[4]

In 1904 Harry was honorably discharged. The same year he married Ida Susan Himrod, a childhood sweetheart he had stayed in touch with.[5] Ida had recently graduated from the New England Conservatory of Oratory in Boston, Massachusetts. After, and before returning to Boise, she traveled extensively with her parents. The two were married in September 1904 at St. Michael's Episcopal Cathedral at the northwest corner of 8th and State streets across from the Capitol building in downtown Boise. The Himrods, who Harry politely styled as "well-off," hosted a lavish wedding for the two, followed by an

---

3   Shellworth. *Travel-Log North Pacific Ocean (1893-1904)*. 1-3.

4   Harry C. Shellworth, annotated note on a newspaper clipping regarding the battle, found in the newspaper clipping file within the Harry C. Shellworth Collection MS-269, Idaho State Historical Society Archives.

5   Harry C. Shellworth, interview by Ralph W. Hidy, 1955, *The Reminiscences of H.C. Shellworth*, Oral History Research Office Weyerhaeuser Project, Forest History Society, 29.

equally extravagant reception at the Himrod's home at the corner of 11th and Jefferson streets. The reception was attended by family and hundreds of friends. The society section of *The Idaho Daily Statesman* dedicated extensive coverage to the wedding, detailing the attire, flowers, music, and attendees. The article referred to the occasion as, "one of the largest and most elaborate weddings ever seen here."[6] The following April, less than two weeks after celebrating her twenty-fifth birthday, Ida became ill and underwent an operation for appendicitis at St. Luke's Hospital.[7] The surgery went well, but a day later she died. Just months after her wedding at St. Michael's, her funeral service was held in the same cathedral, followed by burial at the Pioneer Cemetery.[8]

Grieving Ida's loss, Harry thought about rejoining the transport service, but his family and in-laws asked him to stay in Boise. Harry's father-in-law, Charles Himrod, was a wealthy Idaho businessman who had served as an Idaho Territorial Treasurer and as mayor of Boise. He was well-connected, as was Harry's brother-in-law John Blake, who was married to Ida's older sister, Hattie. Blake was William Borah's law partner before Borah entered full-time public service.[9]

---

6   "The most brilliant social event of the week was the wedding of Miss Ida Himrod and Harry Shellworth," Boise Society Section, *The Idaho Daily Statesman*, 18 September 1904.

7   For unknown reasons Harry later recollected in interviews that Ida died of tuberculosis. However, newspaper articles from *The Idaho Daily Statesman* dated April 8-9, 1905 indicated she died from appendicitis. It is likely she had tuberculosis, too, and that was more dominant in Harry's daily life—hence his recollections.

8   "Mrs. Ida Shellworth Dies At Hospital: Succumbs at St. Luke's From Peritonitis," *The Idaho Daily Statesman*, 9 April 1905.

9   John Blake's wife, Hattie Himrod Blake (July 21, 1878—November 20, 1906), died of tuberculosis and is buried in the Pioneer Cemetery, Boise, Idaho. The law firm was known as Borah, Cavanah, and Blake and existed until 1907. For more information see: Marian C. McKenna, *Borah*, (Ann Arbor, MI: The University of Michigan Press, 1961), 23.

The Himrods and Blake encouraged him to apply for a job opening with the Payette Lumber & Manufacturing Company, a holding of the timber giant Weyerhaeuser, which was buying up timber in the area and was a client of the Borah, Cavanah, and Blake law firm. At the same time, Harry was working at a bank, when he saw a medical physician about his severe cough. The doctor told him he had a defective lung (incipient tuberculosis)—he needed to be out in the open air. This diagnosis, combined with his late-wife's death, led him to take the job with Payette Lumber in late-April 1905. He started as a timber cruiser. Regarding this turn of events Harry commented, "[Thus] began 45 years with the trees." However, he also admitted decades later, "When I went there I didn't know the difference between a pine and a fir and a tamarack or anything else, except they were all evergreen. I didn't even know the tamarack was not an evergreen. But I liked the job. I liked to be outdoors."[10]

Within a short time Harry was promoted and became the land agent in charge of land acquisition and disposal. When asked what other jobs or positions he held during his forty-some years with the company, he joked, "Master Errand Boy" and then explained, "In charge of forest protection and public relations. It was knowing what was going on, and knowing who was doing it, and what yours and their common interests were."[11] Simply put, Harry positioned himself to become a person in the know by getting involved in the industry and over the course of his career was the representative of private timber owners on the Idaho State Forestry Board (1927-1949), served

---

10   Harry C. Shellworth, interview by Ralph W. Hidy, 31

11   Harry C. Shellworth, interview by Ralph W. Hidy, 58-59.

as Civilian Conservation Corps camp coordinator in southern Idaho, vice president of the Western Forestry & Conservation Association (1945-1948), held positions on countless board of directors—from the Idaho State Land Board to road committees—and was a member of the Elks, Masons, City Club, and the Arid Club.

The Payette Lumber & Manufacturing Company was founded in 1902 and merged with a competitor, the Barber Lumber Company, eleven years later to become the Boise Payette Lumber Company. The merger created the southern Idaho interests of the Weyerhaeuser Company, one of the most recognized names in the history of the United States timber industry. Weyerhaeuser had made a fortune in the East and Midwest, harvesting easy-to access and easy-to transport timber. When the resources began to diminish, the company looked westward for inexpensive stands of virgin timber. With high ambitions, the company set its eyes on three distinct areas of Idaho—two north of the Salmon River and one south. However, as Weyerhaeuser historian Ralph W. Hidy noted in *Timber and Men: The Weyerhaeuser Story*, "Nowhere in the Far Northwest did the Weyerhaeuser group cherish brighter hopes at the beginning of the century than in Idaho... But in the forty years after 1900, more disappointment than success was recorded."[12]

At first glance it appeared to be a promising region, as large tracts of inexpensive land with high quality timber were plentiful. Not anticipated were the inaccessibility of the timber, the capital investment

---

12   Ralph W. Hidy, Frank Ernest Hill, and Allan Nevins. *Timber and Men: The Weyerhaeuser Story.* New York: NY, The Macmillan Company, 1963. 248. This book is the definitive source on the history of the Weyerhaeuser Company, especially in regards to the company's activities in Idaho. As is further discussed elsewhere in this writing, Hidy interviewed Shellworth in 1955 as part of his research for the book.

and overall cost of moving the logs to market, and the challenge of the harsh winters. Earlier, the Barber Company, that owned large tracts of timber land in the Boise Basin near Idaho City in the Mores Creek and Grimes Creek drainages, banked on the idea of floating logs down the two creeks to their mill located east of Boise on the Boise River. It proved possible only during times of extremely high water in the spring, and overall was ineffective.

The Payette Company had the same issues with timber along the North Fork of the Payette, since it was unable to move logs effectively down the river to its mill site in Emmett. Doubling down on its investment, Weyerhaeuser sunk considerable capital into transportation systems, as well as two new mills—one at Barber (1915) and one at Emmett (1917). Both mills were linked to rail systems. The Barber Mill relied on the Intermountain Railway that ran from Arrowrock Junction to Centerville, and the Emmett Mill relied on the Oregon Short Line (part of the Union Pacific system) which extended from Emmett to Smiths Ferry and then northward to McCall.[13] The two lines cut through the heart of the Boise Payette Lumber Company private holdings. The company did make money for many decades, but not at the rate anticipated by Weyerhaeuser. The harsh winters combined with the high labor costs and railroad rates put the company's Idaho holdings at an extreme disadvantage compared to

---

13   Portions of the railroad bed are still visible and some have been adopted into rails to trails programs. To support the railroad activities lumber camps and company towns sprang up and moved depending on the areas being logged. Two examples include the sites of Cabarton and MacGregor located south of Cascade. The company town of Cabarton was situated just north of the now popular river access site along the North Fork of the Payette River. The short-lived town was named for Boise Payette Lumber Company president, C.A. Barton. The railroad shaped much of how the towns in the heart of Valley County developed causing many of the established towns prior to the railroad to falter while bringing commerce and prosperity to such towns as Cascade and Donnelly.

competitors in the Midwest. For example, from 1913 to 1931 dividends from earnings on the Boise Payette Lumber Company amounted to only thirty-eight percent of capital invested. Altogether, by 1937 the Weyerhaeuser's Idaho holdings contributed $3,642,000 of distributions to stockholders against $21,744,000 the company had paid out to railroads in freight costs.[14] In spite of the unique and tough challenges of the timber industry in Idaho, collectively Weyerhaeuser also recognized the immense power they held in the state's economy by providing jobs directly and indirectly throughout Idaho.

One advantage Boise Payette had over the other Idaho Weyerhaeuser holdings was the ability to fall and move timber within a relatively close distance to Payette Lake, since it owned large tracts of uncut timber land in the vicinity of the lake. Once skidded down to the lake, the timber was floated to the mill in McCall owned by Carl Brown, a local competitor and a friend of Harry's.[15] Even though the raw logs were sold at a reduced value, it enabled Boise Payette to sell and move logs at times when there was no demand at its own Emmett Mill, or during the shoulder season when transporting the logs to Emmett was not cost-effective. When this was done, Boise Payette simply sold the timber and was not associated with the actual removal or handling of the timber. Harry felt that locals in the McCall area during Boise Payette's early years of operation viewed them as an outsider representing big corporate business. In reviewing the subject,

---

14 Hidy et al, 267.

15 Several of these log chute locations are still evident on Payette Lake, especially when the light is right and the water is clear, big pieces of preserved, clean cut timber can be found entombed on the bottom of the lake. For more information on Brown see: Grace Jordan. *The King's Pines of Idaho: A Story of the Browns of McCall*. Portland, OR: Binfords & Mort Publishers, 1961, and Warren Harrington Brown. *It's Fun to Remember: A King's Pine Autobiography*. Boise, ID: Self-published, 1999.

Harry observed, "[T]he only advice I had up there and stuck with it was that it would be better to sell the little timber we had around Payette Lakes for the reason that if we, a big foreign corporation, cut it, we'd have one hell of a howl from the country about despoiling the Payette Lakes, south Idaho's prime Summer Resort[sic]."[16]

Throughout Harry's career with Boise Payette he substantially grew the company's land holdings, and acquisitions were made using the standard methods of his day. The least used of the approaches was purchasing existing deeded land from a seller. More common tactic in the early 1900s was buying land through the Timber and Stone Act of 1878. It allowed an individual to withdraw up to 160 acres of land unfit for cultivation, but with potential for timber or stone extraction, from the public domain at a cost of $2.50 per acre. For the most part, large lumber companies regarded this as a subversive restriction preventing them from further expanding their holdings because the act limited withdrawn land only to individuals for private use. Unintended outcomes continued for decades after the act was enacted—primarily from large lumber companies that gave incentives to employees to withdraw land in their own name and then flip it to the company for a small profit. It was a legal loophole. Right or wrong, it was a standard practice in land acquisition, and Harry used it as a tool of the trade from 1906 to 1918. Government Land Office Records, combined with Valley County Recorder's Office records, reveal Harry maxed out

---

16   Harry C. Shellworth, interview by Elwood R. Maunder, 1963, *Transcript of Maunder-Shellworth Tapes—Version #1 Unedited*, Forest History Society, 10. There are two transcript versions of the Maunder-Shellworth interviews. Based on conversations with Forest History Society archivists the transcripts were created from the same interview tapes conducted by Maunder in 1963. For clarification as to the source they are referenced as Version #1 and Version #2. Version #1 is lengthier, lacks edits, and includes information not included in the more refined version. Version #2 is more condensed and has been edited.

what he could withdraw under his own name. He also co-withdrew a half a dozen other parcels with unrelated individuals, and then he withdrew additional parcels using his own family member's names. Each property only remained in private ownership a short time before title was transferred to the lumber company.[17]

Another method of timber land acquisition common for the era and successfully used by Harry was purchasing land scrip. To spur economic development in the nineteenth century and early twentieth century the United States allowed local governments and private corporations to withdraw land from the public domain. Typically the buyer would acquire the land in the form of a note and then would sell the right to claim the land to a private investor. It was common that fee simple ownership was only recorded once the land was resold to the end buyer, utilizing a land agent or warrant broker.[18] According to Harry, scrip was the method he used most often to purchase large tracts of the company's holdings. Similar to buying basic deeded property, the scrip was purchased on a per -acre price from four principal companies: Aztec Land and Cattle Company, Northern Pacific Railroad, Moses Scrip Company of Montana, and

---

17 Withdraws under the name Shellworth were traced using the Government Land Office Records, which were then referenced at the Valley County Record's Office for verification of transfer to Boise Payette Lumber Company or Payette Lumber & Manufacturing Company.

18 Definition of "scrip" from *Black's Law Dictionary*, page 1295, "A scrip certificate (or shortly "scrip") is an acknowledgment by the projectors of a company or the issuers of a loan that the person named therein (or more commonly the holder for the time being of the certificate) is entitled to a certain specified number of shares, debentures, bonds, etc. It is usually given in exchange for the letter of allotment, and in its turn is given up for the shares, debentures, or bonds which it represents. Lindl. Partn. 127; Sweet. The term has also been applied in the United States to warrants or other like orders drawn on a municipal treasury (Alma v. Guaranty Sav. Bank, 60 Fed. 207, 8 C. C. A. 564,) to certificates showing the holder to be entitled to a certain portion or allotment of public or state lands, (Wait v. State Land Office Com'r, 87 Mich. 353, 49 N. W. 600,) and to the fraction."

Utah and Idaho Land and Livestock Company. Players in the land scrip business sold basic timber lands across the West at or near the market value of other comparable deeded land, or as Harry said, "It [the land] was fee simple—sky high and earth deep." However, the more basic lands he purchased were very different from those sites having potential for the selection of dam sites, resorts, or oil well development. These properties were sold at three and four times what the speculators owning the actual scrip paid for them. Of all the scrip companies, Harry purchased the most land from Aztec Land and Cattle Company over a several year period beginning in 1909, and it eventually added it up to approximately 55,000 acres.[19] Much of this land was located near McCall and scattered along the low ridgelines of Payette Lake, as well as one key parcel with major lake frontage.[20]

Along with his job at the lumber company, while having a pulse on all things forestry in the state, came the position of legislative lobbyist. First and foremost Harry lobbied directly for only one of the Weyerhaeuser affiliated companies—Boise Payette. Although, if there were no conflicts of interest with Boise Payette, he actively lobbied for decades for the other two Weyerhaeuser holding companies

---

19 Harry C. Shellworth, interview by Elwood R. Maunder, 1963, *Transcript of Maunder-Shellworth Tapes—Version #2 Edited*, Forest History Society, 3-4. There are two transcript versions of the Maunder-Shellworth interviews. Based on conversations with Forest History Society archivists the transcripts were created from the same interview tapes conducted by Maunder in 1963. For clarification as to the source they are referenced as Version #1 and Version #2. Version #1 is lengthier, lacks edits, and includes information not included in the more refined version. Version #2 is more condensed and has been edited

20 Many of the Aztec Land and Cattle Company withdraws were traced using the Government Land Office Records, which were then referenced at the Valley County Record's Office for verification of transfer to Boise Payette Lumber Company or Payette Lumber and Manufacturing Company.

in northern Idaho, as well as several other big lumber companies. When asked if he was paid for his lobbying work for the other companies, Harry admitted that he did accept "gifts." The "gifts" usually arrived around Christmas in the form of payments ranging from $250 to $500 per company, "It wasn't an obligation. I never asked for it. They would write [me] down their [Boise/southern Idaho] and ask me to do so-and-so for them, and I did it to their satisfaction, and it was just a return."[21]

With his career established, Harry began dating a young lady, Stella B. Whitney. As with everything else in Harry's life, it was a unique courtship he later dubbed the "Courtship Shadows." Stella's father, Eugene L. Whitney (1855-1911) was the warden of the Idaho State Penitentiary located north of Warm Springs Avenue at the eastern edge of Boise. By the summer of 1907, the two were engaged, which happened to be the same time as the three-part trial concerning the assassination of former Idaho Governor Frank Steunenberg.[22]

Harry Shellworth had met and become acquainted with Steunenberg when Harry was a page in the first state legislative session. Early in the session the two happened to meet at a downtown candy store while Harry was buying a nickel bag of strawberry taffy and Steunenberg was buying his regular bag of vanilla taffy. The two struck up a conversation and for the remainder of the 1890 legislative session, Steunenberg supplied Harry with his weekly taffy ration.

---

21   Harry C. Shellworth, interview by Elwood R. Maunder, Version #2, 17.

22   For more information on the history of the Steunenberg trial see: J. Anthony Lukas. *Big Trouble: A Murder in a Small Western Town Sets Off a Struggle For the Soul of America*. New York, NY: Simon & Schuster, 1997.

Remembering their brief friendship Harry stated, "Steunenberg and I were great friends; as a boy knows a man, he was a very kindly man."[23] Five years after leaving office Steunenberg was killed by a bomb rigged to the side gate of his Caldwell house. Within a short time Harry Orchard was arrested for the crime. Initially he denied involvement, but eventually confessed to being hired as an assassin by Big Bill Haywood, the general secretary of the Western Federation of Miners.

Each day of the trial, Orchard was transported in the warden's personal open automobile to the Ada County Courthouse, along with a driver and two guards. Stella was the driver and when they arrived at the courthouse, two additional guards joined the group and Stella turned the car over to them. Not wanting to sit around the courthouse all day, Harry would frequently meet her and take her to lunch. When finished, he walked her back to the courthouse. Expecting a possible attempt on Orchard's life, the state hired detectives with the Thiel Agency of Spokane, Washington, to watch all movements connected to the trial. Given the pattern of Stella and Harry's regular meetings after Orchard was brought to the courthouse from the penitentiary, the detectives, unknown to Harry, began following him.[24] However, he did not learn about this until a year later.

In April 1908 Harry and Stella married. Governor Frank Gooding and his family were guests. At the reception, Gooding congratulated the newlyweds and said when you are back from your honeymoon stop by my office for a visit, "I will let you read carbon copies of

---

23   Harry C. Shellworth, interview by Ralph W. Hidy, 44.

24   H.C. Shellworth. *Courtship Shadows*, (1963). Shellworth Family Collection.

three 'Shadow' reports of your courtship." Apparently the detectives thought Harry was a potential assassin. When the reports came across the Governor's desk he commented, "I will vouch for Mr. Shellworth, you need not 'shadow' him anymore."[25]

---

25   H.C. Shellworth. *Courtship Shadows,* (1963). Shellworth Family Collection.

HARRY SHELLWORTH ON HIS EIGHTEENTH BIRTHDAY.
(Shellworth Family Collection)

STELLA WHITNEY, RIGHT, HARRY'S SECOND WIFE,
AND SISTER HELEN AT THE IDAHO STATE
PENITENTIARY WARDEN'S RESIDENCE, 1907.
(Shellworth Family Collection)

2

SITPA

From the look-out on Shafer Butte, 7,500 feet up among the mountain of Southern Idaho, the earth falls away on every side like a crumpled parchment. In one direction it is cracked and browned by centuries of sunburn, and blank as far as the eye can see. That is a distance of sixty or seventy miles, but if you could look from here to Mexico the prospect would be much the same: sand with a fuzz of sagebrush, mountains bald save patches of hairlike dry grass that flowers in its season and turns into patches of varicolored, faded velvet ruffled by the wind.
—ANNE O'HARE MCCORMICK
An American Epic in Sand and Flame (1931)

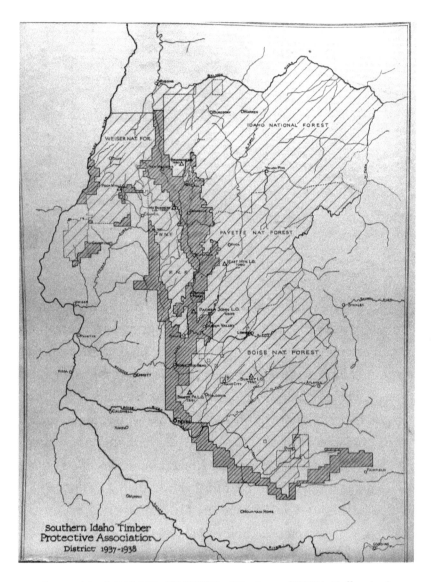

LANDS PROTECTED BY SITPA, SHADED. *(SITPA Collection)*

Early in Harry's career with the Payette Lumber & Manufacturing Company he found himself fighting a fire on Dry Buck Summit three miles northwest of the confluence of the North Fork and South Fork of the Payette rivers in an effort to protect valuable private timber holdings. This led to one of Harry's greatest contributions to the state of Idaho that remains today—the creation of Southern Idaho Timber Protective Association (SITPA). While on the fire, he met another firefighter. Remembering the encounter, Harry recalled, "He was soot-blackened and fire-grimed," but as the pair drew nearer to one another Harry suddenly recognized him as Guy B. Mains with the US Forest Service.[26]

The two put the fire out and then sat down to visit. The conversation led to a lengthy discussion of the need for a cooperative fire prevention organization that would encompass not only federal lands, but also private and state lands. Of one mind, in 1908 the two essentially began a gentleman's agreement. The arrangement formed a co-operative among timber stakeholders who were willing to work together to fight fire, with the idea that the costs would be paid on the basis of their proportionate acreage of land that burned.[27] The informal agreement worked for three years and was eventually backed in 1911 by state legislation and labeled the Southern Idaho Co-operative Fire Protective Association—Shellworth was appointed secretary manager. The official name was changed in 1919 to Southern Idaho Timber Protective

---

26 Harry C. Shellworth, interview by Elwood R. Maunder, Version #2, 15.

27 From 1908 to 1910 the stakeholders included: The state of Idaho, Payette Lumber & Manufacturing Company, as well as the Boise and Payette National Forests. Depending on the source, earlier dates referencing another cooperative agreement pre-dating 1908 were sometimes used in SITPA publications, likely in an effort to establish more credibility or predate other timber protective associations. The dates used herein are the most consistent and commonly used in a multitude of historical documents.

Association (SITPA).[28] Seven TPAs (Clearwater, Coeur d'Alene, Pend Oreille, Pine Creek, Potlatch, Priest Lake, and Southern Idaho) were established in Idaho and eventually the concept spread nationwide. Originally unique to Idaho, TPAs became known as "The Idaho Idea." Early TPAs helped push Congress to pass the Weeks Law in 1911 and the Clark McNary Act in 1924. These laws provide federal funds for private timber owners to aid in wildland fire protection.

At the helm of SITPA, Harry created a culture within the organization very different from those found in other land management agencies in the same line of work. At SITPA he fostered a family atmosphere where everyone worked together, from the fire warden and administrative staff to the firefighters in the field and to the men and women staffing the lookout stations. There was no clocking in and clocking out—people just did what needed to be done. Harry valued having the "best" working for him and in an industry where seasonal workers were usually hired during the height of fire season, he found year-round employment for most of his staff, thus keeping the most knowledgeable and skilled people on the payroll for years. Harry boasted about the Association's personnel in the SITPA annual reports. Illustrating his commitment to his employees, he wrote in one report, "Because of the necessity of almost daily contact with the public—both by patrolmen and lookouts—the diversity of our annual improvement plans, and the unusual public interest in every phase of our work, it is necessary that we not only secure a type of forest worker capable of rendering the Association efficient service, but also with a personality that will help us secure the understanding and confidence

---

28   Harry C. Shellworth. *Annual Report: Southern Idaho Timber Protective Association 1929.* SITPA, 1929, 7. On file at the SITPA office in McCall, ID.

we so earnestly desire, of the citizens of Idaho. Under such conditions, and taking the seasonal limitations of the employment into consideration, we feel we should be pardoned if we exhibit some pride in the field personnel of this Association. We admit such pride."[29]

The Association established a headquarters on land provided by the Boise Payette Lumber Company at a midway point among members' land at Smiths Ferry along the North Fork of the Payette River and Highway 15 (now Highway 55) between Boise and McCall. Considerable money was invested in the site in 1927 with the development of a beautifully crafted log residence to suit the needs of a fulltime fire warden, along with several outbuildings to house crews and firefighting equipment.[30] The buildings dating to this era were constructed by Finnish log experts Gust Lapinoja and John Heikkila from Long Valley.[31] The architecture and finish of the main cabin is often described as "rustic," which is a misnomer. The work done by these two Finnish log axman was anything but rustic as each log was scribed, fitted, and dovetailed at each corner. The quality of their work was unrivaled.[32]

---

29   Harry C. Shellworth. *Annual Report: Southern Idaho Timber Protective Association 1929.* SITPA, 1929, 16. On file at the SITPA office in McCall, ID.

30   Harry C. Shellworth. *Annual Report: Southern Idaho Timber Protective Association 1927.* SITPA, 1927. Harry C. Shellworth Collection MS-269, Idaho State Historical Society Archives.

31   Finnish construction in the McCall and Long Valley area of Valley County is not uncommon as many Finns were the first to settle in the Valley. The first Finnish settlers arrived in the 1890s and were typically farmers. Most of the early Finns moved from Pendleton, Oregon, in the 1890s and were later joined by Finns from Wyoming mining towns. For more information see: Merle A. Reinikka. *Finnish Settlers of Long Valley, Idaho.* Portland, OR: Finnish American Historical Society of the West, 1990.

32   Frank W. Eld. *Finnish Log Construction—The Art: The Story of Finnish Log Construction in America.* Donnelly, ID: F.W. Eld, 2013.

To protect much of the land under SITPA's jurisdiction, the Association opted to develop several fire detection points as fire lookout facilities. The idea of fire lookouts was fairly new when the Association was formed. Early lookout facilities were generally located on prominent high points, such as ridges or mountaintops overlooking fire prone areas. In the beginning, lookout facilities were visited daily or weekly after a lightning storm or during times of high fire danger. But as the lookout system developed into a network funded by both private, state, and federal agencies they realized the sooner a fire could be spotted, the more quickly it could be extinguished, thus minimizing the fire and costs. With this in mind, permanent buildings with living quarters were constructed on mountaintops across the United States. Due to the mountainous terrain and abundance of timber, more than 1,000 fire lookout locations were used in Idaho, more than any other state. The development of the fire lookout stations began as modest camps and slowly evolved into small permanent buildings enabling a lookout to live at their location for a few months during fire season. Due to the high altitude and remote locations, most of the early buildings were constructed of native materials that could be gathered near the site. To ease the challenges associated with constructing lookout buildings in remote locations, the US Forest Service developed precut kits that could be packed on horses and mules and then assembled in place. Forest Service facilities were generally basic and utilitarian in design and materials.

In comparison to the Forest Service, the SITPA fire lookout facilities were anything but "basic" or "utilitarian," as Harry insisted on the finest. To him the Association's fire lookout facilities were more than just a place to detect fires, they were a symbol of SITPA and provided an excellent opportunity to share its mission and purpose with the public. As a result, his interpretation of what a fire lookout facility should be was fairly elaborate. In the beginning, SITPA built lookout stations on Brundage Mountain (1914) and East Mountain (1914). Their network was then expanded with the construction of lookouts at Packer John (1929), and Shafer Butte (1927). SITPA also worked jointly with the Forest Service on operational funding for facilities at Sunset Peak (1930) and Peck Mountain (1919), which served both private and National Forest lands. The lookouts were strategically placed to view private timber stands, and timber stands threatened or impacted by insects and disease common to the era, such as pine white butterfly, spruce budworm, tussock moth, and mistletoe.

Ironically, the Association, primarily made up of members who viewed forests in board-feet, recognized the most fire-prone areas were those that had been heavily cut-over and left with slash. Members such as Harry also recognized the negative environmental impacts associated with poor logging techniques of the past and in 1929 he wrote in the annual report, "Because of the abuses that have accumulated over a period of nearly fifty years and which have only recently become apparent to the public mind, we have problems in forest protection work that need constructive thought, co-operation of the interests and educational work, of high integrity, intelligently conceived. To this end the interest, understanding and confidence of the Idaho citizen must be obtained through his belief in the ability, integrity, and permanency of our efforts. In such an effort this Association will endeavor to be of real service in forest protection and reforestation in Idaho."[33] As a subtle conservationist and timber

---

33   Harry C. Shellworth. *Annual Report: Southern Idaho Timber Protective Association 1929.* SITPA, 1929. 16. On file at the SITPA office in McCall, ID.

industry advocate, Harry spun a positive view on the large clear-cuts found near some of the Association's lookouts by calling them "pioneer cuttings," taking the focus away from the sea of stumps caused by out-of-date timber practices and converting them into historical points of interest to visitors.[34] Under Harry's direction, SITPA was the first to coin and use the phrase "Keep Idaho Green." In an annotated note regarding the slogan, Harry scribbled in a 1929 copy of the Association's annual report, "The 1923 report was the 1st time this was used...whether or not it was original is a question; however, it was original with us. HCS."[35] In the Forest History Society archives, Harry's reference predates any other similar "green program" by seventeen years with the first official recognition given to the state of Washington in 1940, and to Idaho with a state issued program in 1946.[36]

The first lookout facility at Brundage Mountain consisted of a small log cabin built of peeled whitebark pine logs for the living quarters, and the observation platform was crude scaffolding built around a topped tree that served as the firefinder stand. Five years later, in 1919, a larger live-in lookout, also built of logs, was added to the north. The new 18' x 18' two-story structure featured a viewing area on the second floor and a living area on the first floor, fancy compared to other early lookouts. The same design had been used for the construction of the East Mountain Lookout in 1914. The lookouts were not

---

34 Harry C. Shellworth. *Annual Report: Southern Idaho Timber Protective Association 1929.* SITPA, 1929. 18. On file at the SITPA office in McCall, ID.

35 Harry C. Shellworth. *Annual Report: Southern Idaho Timber Protective Association 1929.* SITPA, 1929. 8. Harry C. Shellworth Collection MS-269, Idaho State Historical Society Archives.

36 Eben Lehman. "Forgotten Characters from Forest History: 'The Guberif.'" *Peeling Back the Bark: Exploring the collection, acquisitions, and treasures of the Forest History Society,* January 2011.

only unique in their spaciousness, but they also featured a "bird cage" lightning grounding system found nowhere else. The same overall design of building and lightning grounding system was then carried over to Shafer Butte and Packer John. The Shafer Butte Lookout was particularly unique, since Harry again hired Gust Lapinoja and John Heikkila to construct it. The construction techniques were like those used at the Smiths Ferry headquarters, using full dove-tail corners and fine Finnish carpentry throughout.

Shortly after establishing a fine network of fire lookout stations for the Association, Harry attended a business meeting in northern Idaho. During the meeting, E.C. Rettig, a land agent with Potlatch Forests, Inc., one of the Weyerhaeuser's northern Idaho holding companies, upbraided Harry about the costs of his lookouts, questioning whether or not they had been worth it. In an annotated note about the event Harry commented, "He [Rettig] was sure all present would like to know what 'the correct costs of my Gold Lace Lookouts were.' My response, 'I don't know—but the PR value and dividends are so high I never bothered to check, but I would look it up.' I thanked him for suggesting a good name for them."[37] Taking it one step further, Harry sent him a personal Christmas card at the end of the year with a photograph of the Brundage Mountain Lookout. Rettig responded with, "Dear Harry: I want to take this occasion to congratulate you on the novel Christmas card which you sent. You surely must have spent considerable time in picking out two trees, such as are shown on the right and left hand corners of your card. The center view is a

---

37   Harry C. Shellworth, annotated note written in the margins of a letter from E.C. Rettig. 30 December 1931. Harry C. Shellworth Collection MS-269, Idaho State Historical Society Archives.

very beautiful picture also, in fact it is nice enough to frame."[38] Harry
embraced Rettig's ribbing and from the time of that meeting, Harry
referred to his fire detection stations as "Gold Lace Lookouts."

In addition to the money spent on the fire lookouts, SITPA
invested considerable capital in building automobile roads to Shafer
Butte and Brundage Mountain, which were closest to major population centers. In Harry's opinion the only portion of the public that
could access lookouts without roads were people, "[O]n shoe leather or
horseback."[39] He envisioned having roads to each of the Association's
lookouts, but the Great Depression restricted the progress for several
years, leaving East Mountain and Packer John accessible only by trail
until the mid-1930s.[40] However, the roads built to the lookouts served
multiple purposes, since they were good firebreaks, forest patrol
roads, and served as scenic roads for the public, luring them directly
to the heart of Harry's public relation campaign. He explained, "I put
all that white paint on them so that when people drove through Long
Valley in the summer they'd see the sun shining on the white lookout
buildings from the valley and they'd get curious and go up the road.
And when they got up there they found something that appealed
to their sense of calmness and security, and beauty, and also forest
protection and permanency."[41] Furthermore, Harry could justify his

---

38 E.C. Rettig. Letter to Harry C. Shellworth, Land Agent Boise Payette Lumber Company. 30
    December 1930. Harry C. Shellworth Collection MS-269, Idaho State Historical Society Archives.

39 Harry C. Shellworth, interview by Elwood R. Maunder, Version #2, 30.

40 A number of the early roads built by the Association were nothing more than improve-
    ments or conversions of the former logging railroad beds used by the Boise Payette Lumber
    Company or its predecessors. For example see page 29 of the SITPA annual report.

41 Fire lookout historians have deduced that not all SITPA lookout buildings were initially paint-
    ed white. Based on historic images some of the lookout structures were stained in natural
    browns, while others were even painted with reflective silver paint.

expensive lookouts because he earned strong public support, and it increased the image of SITPA, "Those Gold Lace Lookouts built up favorable sentiment towards our work down here in South Idaho, and sometimes even brought a favorable comparison with the federal government work. School children, Campfire Girls, and Boy Scouts went up there, and wrote essays about their trips for local papers."[42]

Harry was also accomplished at attracting journalists to write articles in local and regional newspapers about SITPA lookouts through his many friends and acquaintances in the newspaper business. His Gold Lace Lookouts were often featured in the Sunday editions of *The Idaho Daily Statesman*, encouraging the public to drop by for a visit. He was clever in personalizing the stations with a focus on the individuals who staffed them, giving the public another thing to remember. Two of the more publicized characters to staff the Gold Lace Lookouts in the Progressive Era were Johnny Hargrave and Mrs. William Moore, who Harry referred to in SITPA literature and in publicity stories as the "lady lookout." Her actual name was Violet Eva Hills and she married William J. Moore. The two worked several years in the 1920s and early 1930s for SITPA on East Mountain and Shafer Butte. They left the lookout life for fulltime farming in Malheur County, Oregon, where they raised several children. William died in July 1977 and Violet in February 1994. Hargrave worked for SITPA for more than a dozen years as a fire lookout on various stations, but mainly Brundage Mountain. He was born in Silver City, Idaho, and died in Boise in January 1940 at the age of seventy-five. Prior to being

---

42   Harry C. Shellworth, interview by Ralph W. Hidy, 67-68.

a lookout, he was a miner, lumberjack and soldier. According to a tribute to him in *The Idaho Daily Statesman*, Harry stated, "He was one of our best lookouts, probably the best. He was always alert, on the job, and had an all-around keen woods sense. When it came to animals and birds he was a whiz. He made pets of squirrels and all sorts of birds that frequented his lookouts. At one time I remember seeing at least twenty squirrels swarming about him as he fed them by hand."[43]

Harry realized that competent photographs accompanying the newspaper articles caught the attention of readers far more than text or headline. From the 1920s through the early 1940s, Harry frequently hired his close friend and Boise-based professional photographer, Ansgar Johnson, Sr., to photograph the activities of SITPA, along with his many outdoor adventures with prominent businessmen and politicians. In 1911 Ansgar, and his father Jens Peter, opened Johnson & Son, a photography shop in downtown Boise. The Johnson's principal work was portraits, but by the mid-1920s Ansgar had earned a reputation as a highly regarded and gifted landscape photographer; having grasped the crucial role of light and balance in his compositions.[44] In addition to his portrait and landscape work, he also worked as the staff news photographer for local papers in Idaho and adjacent areas in the Northwest that served as feeders to big national papers such as *The New York Times*. In the 1920s and 1930s it was fairly common to see Johnson & Son photographs printed in the Sunday edition of *The Times* in the photogravure sections. Harry regarded Ansgar

---

43   "Veteran Forest Lookout Ends Career," *The Idaho Daily Statesman*, 28 January 1940.

44   Carolyn Johnson. Personal Communication with Richard H. Holm, Jr. 10 February 2020.

as "Idaho's most efficient photographer...Johnson's photographic work was superb."[45] And as an outcome of their friendship, Harry kept a portfolio of beautiful photographs to enhance the work and efforts of SITPA. Ansgar's daughter in-law, Carolyn Johnson, commented, "Ansgar was the natural to fill this role and subsequently Ansgar took more and more pictures of Idaho's natural wonders and in the process earned recognition as Idaho's de facto official landscape photographer."[46]

Another distinction established by SITPA was the guest register. Each lookout kept a guestbook for visitors to sign including where they were from. They were popular with the public because signing provided grounds for conversation with the lookout staff. For many visitors and families, the Gold Lace Lookouts, extending from the ridges and mountaintops of the Boise Basin through the Payette Lakes region, became annual destinations for picnics and camping trips. Repeat visitors enjoyed finding their signatures or family and friend's signatures from years past in the registers. In addition, SITPA was collecting data to target a specific audience and share with them the Association's fire prevention and conservation ethics. In the 1931 SITPA annual report the statistics for the year revealed, "[O]ver 4,000 people visited these stations, 80 percent or more being from the Snake

---

45   Harry C. Shellworth, interview by Elwood R. Maunder, Version #2, 34.

46   C. Johnson. Personal Communication. Ansgar Sr. married Roxy McMillian and they had three sons, Ansgar Jr., Peter, and McMillian. Ansgar Jr. was brought into the family business and the studio was located on the top floor of the Sonna Building in downtown Boise. Unfortunately, the studio caught fire in September 1951 and Johnson & Sons lost all of the negatives and prints, as well as all of their equipment. The only Johnson & Sons photographs in existence today are those prints from private collections. The business was rebuilt and Ansgar Sr. retired in the mid-1960s. He and Roxie spent their retirement years splitting their time between McCall and Palm Desert, California. Ansgar Sr. died in 1981 at the age of eighty-eight.

River and Boise Valley irrigation projects and towns. Many names of national and state importance were signed in these registers—US Foresters, National Forest Service officials, officials of the US Land Office, officials of the US Department of the Interior, US Senators and Congressmen, other state and federal officials, editors of newspapers and magazines."[47] Furthermore, "The District of Columbia, twenty-eight states, England, Scotland, China, Canada and Europe were represented on the registers."[48] One year SITPA collected addresses in the register and sent personal Christmas cards to everyone who had signed-in at one of the organization's lookouts.

Harry even used the SITPA lookouts to help influence politicians by holding informal meetings at their locations. One example was at the Brundage Lookout (c. 1925) when Shellworth, struggling to gain support on a cooperative forestry bill, knew that without the backing of the Idaho Editorial Association, would fail. To gain their support, he organized a buffet breakfast for the Association at the lookout. Everyone enjoyed the meeting so much that Harry had to send some of his staff down to McCall for lunch fixings and beverages. By the end of the day, all of the members of the Idaho Editorial Association voiced full support.

---

47 Harry C. Shellworth. *Annual Report: Southern Idaho Timber Protective Association 1931*. SITPA, 1931. 8. Harry C. Shellworth Collection MS-269, Idaho State Historical Society Archives.

48 Southern Idaho Timber Protective Association Annual Reports from 1927 to 1931 on file at the SITPA Office, McCall, ID.

EAST MOUNTAIN LOOKOUT, 1920S. MR. AND MRS. WILLIAM MOORE,
LEFT AND SITPA CHIEF FIRE WARDEN ART COONROD, RIGHT.
(Johnson & Son/Shellworth Family Collection)

BRUNDAGE MOUNTAIN LOOKOUT, 1920S.
JOHNNY HARGRAVE AND GUEST.
(*Dudley Family Collection/Central Idaho Historical Museum*)

SHAFER BUTTE LOOKOUT, 1929, VIOLET MOORE. *(SITPA Collection)*

SMITHS FERRY SITPA HEADQUARTERS, 1920S.
(Johnson & Son/SITPA Collection)

ANSGAR JOHNSON, SR., 1930S. HARRY'S FRIEND
AND PHOTOGRAPHER. *(Carolyn Johnson)*

SMITHS FERRY HEADQUARTERS, 1930S.
(Johnson & Son/SITPA Collection)

INTERMOUNTAIN REGIONAL FOREST PROTECTION
BOARD, SHAFER BUTTE, JULY 1929. HARRY FRONT
ROW, THIRD FROM LEFT. *(SITPA Collection)*

SHAFER BUTTE FORESTRY GATHERING 1930S.
BACK ROW SECOND FROM LEFT ART COONROD (SITPA)
AND HARRY, THIRD FROM LEFT.
FOUR MEMBERS OF US SENATE FORESTRY
COMMITTEE FRONT ON RIGHT.
(Johnson & Son/SITPA Collection)

SHAFER BUTTE FORESTRY MEETING, 1929.
BACK ROW LEFT TO RIGHT: C.B. MORSE (USFS), US WEATHER
BUREAU STAFF, ARCHIE RYAN (US DEPARTMENT OF INTERIOR),
I.H. NASH (IDAHO STATE LAND COMMISSIONER),
H.C. BALDRIDGE (IDAHO GOVERNOR),
C.A. BARTON (G.M. BOISE PAYETTE LUMBER COMPANY).
FRONT ROW LEFT TO RIGHT:
ART COONROD (SITPA) AND HARRY.
(SITPA Collection)

3

SUCCESS AMONG THE NEW DEALERS AND THE CCC

The achievement of the CCC in Idaho was considerable,
not only in providing relief and local expenditures, but also
in lasting accomplishments...The CCC was especially well
administered in Idaho, and there seems to have been little
friction or misunderstanding between federal administrators
and Idahoans. Local political jealousies over hiring
provided the only real controversies in the Idaho ECW.
—MICHAEL P. MALONE
C. Ben Ross: And the New Deal in Idaho (1970)

As the secretary and manager of SITPA, and while promised regularity in the lumber company, Harry found himself embroiled in state and national politics—particularly on policy tied to forestry initiatives. His network of acquaintances and friends grew and so did Harry's excellent reputation. From the start, Harry was a natural "people person." He was personable in conversation and comfortable whether he was in a casual social setting or in a formal meeting. He always offered a firm handshake when greeting someone, looked people in the eye, treated all people equally, and called them by their first name, even if it was someone he had only met once. Summing up Harry's character, the Ansgar Johnson, Sr. family referred to him as a "hale-fellow-well-met." By his fifties Harry appeared stout, distinctive face, with blue eyes, in a slight smile, lightly suntanned skin and always dapperly dressed. He was meeting with Idaho's governors and senators regarding company business; he developed personal friendships with many of them—Idaho Senator William Borah, Governor H.C. Baldridge, Governor Ben Ross, and Governor C.A. Bottolfsen. Harry, a staunch member of the GOP, thrived in the conservative politics of the Progressive Era. As that period was overshadowed by the more liberal New Deal, one would have expected his influence to wane, but for the gregarious Shellworth the new political climate only strengthened his influence at state and federal levels, because he had the ability to work in the background and reach across party aisles. In respect to his political work, Harry remarked in 1963, "I can't tell you exactly why I started to do it [politics] except I had an interest in people. I like people. I don't think there's anything in the world more interesting to watch, but I have no desire whatever to push anybody around and nobody's going to push me around."[49] A few years earlier on the same topic Harry explained to historian Ralph W. Hidy, "Everyone talks about politics in the same way, but I've seen it and learned it...

---

49   Harry C. Shellworth, interview by Ralph W. Hidy, 11.

when you bring it right down and forget all the little human selfish-ness and leave out all the sanctimonious posing, politics is simply the science of harmonizing the interests of the most people...whatever they may be, sons-of-bitches or priests."[50]

In part, some of this influence was generated by happenstance, as in April 1933 when Governor Ross, who was a Democrat, called upon his Republican friend Harry to go to Washington, D.C., concerning the establishment of the Civilian Conservation Corps (CCC). Designed by the Roosevelt administration as part of the Great Depression eco-nomic recovery, the CCC was a public work-relief program aimed at putting unemployed unmarried men (ages seventeen to twenty-eight) back to work. The CCC was structured similarly to the military where enrollees lived in camps, but instead of training or fighting a war, the men performed manual labor related to the conservation of the nation's natural resources in rural areas. According to Harry's 1960s reminis-cences of the trip, he had a personal letter from Governor Ross saying in effect he was the governor's personal representative, and therefore the state's sole representative on the matter, even though others were there representing Idaho. The others were described by Harry as, "[I]nfants back in Washington." He then further clarified, "I'd been there for years and years...And I had made acquaintances particularly in the West and the South, and one or two in the North. And I was very lucky, just put it that way. I just had wonderful success."[51]

Through Harry's prior experiences in Washington, he knew many of the key players involved with the development of the CCC program.

---

50   Harry C. Shellworth, interview by Ralph W. Hidy, 13.

51   Harry C. Shellworth, interview by Michael P. Malone, 1964, Forest History Society, 10-11.

As the final weeks of the meetings drew to a close, representatives from each state were to submit detailed proposals regarding the number of CCC camps their state wanted, along with the location of each. Harry consulted with several friends at the meetings and spent all night drawing up his proposal, finishing at four in the morning. At nine o'clock Idaho's proposal was the first plan on the table for review by the nine USFS regional foresters, and it was also the first plan approved. At the end of the CCC meetings, Idaho had the largest number of CCC camps of any state west of the Mississippi, except California. Harry admitted that much of his success was to the credit of his friends who he had consulted, many of whom were the regional foresters making the decisions.

From the onset, the Idaho CCC program was divided into three districts with administrative offices somewhat centrally located within each of the respective districts: Spokane/Lewiston, Pocatello, and Boise. Each district then had its own specific camps with offices, mess halls, and barracks. Based on the assignments of the camps, they were split into various categories depending on the related agencies or tasks. In Idaho, a majority of the camps were designated "F" for the US Forest Service, for the simple reason that much of the federal land in the state was part of the National Forest system. The next largest group was "G" or "DG," referring to the Department of Grazing.[52] Other common designations were "S" for the State of Idaho, "P" for Private, "SP" for State Park, "SCS" for the Soil Conservation Service and "BR" for the Bureau of Reclamation. Idaho had only one State Park (SP) camp but a large number of "S" and "P" designated camps.

---

52   The Department of Grazing was later merged by the Truman Administration with the General Land Office to become the Bureau of Land Management.

The private camps were often tied to the timber protection associations around the state.

The supervisors or coordinators of these camps held a powerful position since they essentially controlled the projects and money being funneled into the struggling economies of rural Idaho through the program. Given Harry's position with the lumber company and SITPA, combined with his knowledge and skills, it was no surprise that when he returned from the April 1933 meetings in Washington, Governor Ross appointed him as a coordinator of nine camps within the Boise District. Over the course of the program these original camps changed, with some closing and others opening, depending on the location of the projects. The camps under Harry's supervision consisted of both "S" and "P" designations with camp locations at Tamarack, Meadows, McCall, Cascade, Smiths Ferry, Centerville, Placerville, Holcomb, and one near Shafer Butte along the Boise Ridge.[53] Statewide there were 163 camps, each lasting for an average of three years. Of these camps 109 were F, twenty were S, nine were P. The remainder fell under the other categories. Over the nine year period nationwide, more than two-and-a-half-million young men were enrolled, filling 4,500 camps. It is estimated the young men planted more than two billion trees, labored six-and-a half-million man-days fighting fires, and actively traversed twenty-one million acres of forests in conservation efforts to help fight plant disease and insect damage. The nation as a whole benefited from the enrollees work, but the enrollees also benefited because they acquired skills through educational programs ranging from basic literacy to

---

53   "Report Lauds Forest Work: CCC Given Credit for Preventing Damaging Fires in Local Areas," *The Idaho Daily Statesman*, 6 February 1934.

truck-driving, and in some cases young men earned high school-and college-equivalent diplomas.[54]

Although the program was celebrated by many, it had its critics. Elers Koch, a seasoned forester with the Forest Service based in Montana and northern Idaho, who worked with the CCC camps in his area on National Forests was one of them. In his memoir, *Forty Years a Forester*, Koch wrote, "On the whole the boys were babied too much for their own good or the good of the work. It cost approximately $1,200 a year to maintain a CCC boy in the camps, and in my best judgement the work accomplished per boy was equivalent to about $300 to $400 in regular appropriations."[55] Koch figured two of his well-trained thirty-man crews could outperform any full two-hundred-man CCC camp. He believed the Works Progress Administration, another New Deal Program aimed at getting men back to work, had the same shortcomings as the CCC program. In his opinion the programs were too heavily weighted toward physical labor, which effectively accomplished only low-priority jobs. In essence, he thought it would be more effective and cost efficient to focus on higher priority projects by providing trained and skilled laborers with machinery, instead of hand tools such as shovels.[56]

After the first season of operation in 1933, Harry wrote a report to Governor Ross detailing the activities of his nine camps. In tune with the objectives of putting men back to work, Harry was a practical man, but also recognized the inefficiencies critiqued by

---

54   Judith Austin. "CCC in Idaho." *Idaho Yesterdays 27* (Fall 1983), 13-17.

55   Elers Koch. *Forty Years A Forester: 1903-1943.* Missoula, MT: Mountain Press Publishing Company, 1998. 183-84.

56   Koch, 184-85

like-minded professional foresters such as Koch. Although Harry also had opinions about men such as Koch, who held a master's degree from the prestigious Yale School of Forestry, he said, "[T] hose degree boys are pretty tight you know, they won't stand for 'us Mustangs' at all. We can be 'notable woodsmen' in their vocabulary, but 'Foresters'—never."[57] For a "Mustang" the solution was simple—provide the CCC boys equipment. So in his report to Ross he suggested, "Greater accomplishment in proportion to company manpower would be obtained with full complement of heavy equipment for each camp, adequate to the project for that camp."[58] As Harry expected, his recommendation was met with resistance from other CCC administrators in the Boise District, as it posed a potential threat to manual labor, and thus a reduction in men. However, he persevered. The specifics are not clear, but among his personal archives are photographs of a bulldozer with the caption, "The illegal Caterpillar tractor. The damn bureaucrats said I couldn't have any heavy equipment. I told them where they could go—they didn't hear me. I got the Cats." It would appear when an inspection was planned, the Cat was hidden as inferred from another note next to the picture in Shellworth's handwriting, "I ran the Cat off into the brush and gave the boys shovels and rakes until the inspectors left. They know less about road work than I do about preaching."[59]

---

57   Harry C. Shellworth, interview by Ralph W. Hidy, 72

58   Harry C. Shellworth. Report of Work by Southern Idaho Civilian Conservation Corps Camps to Governor C. Ben Ross. February 1934. Harry C. Shellworth Collection MS-269, Idaho State Historical Society Archives.

59   CCC in Idaho Collection MS-683, Idaho State Historical Society Archives.

The position of the CCC coordinator was to some degree an honorary appointment from Governor Ross and was unpaid. After a few seasons Harry felt his job with the Boise Payette Lumber Company was suffering, even though he had the support of his boss, Jack Moon. Plus, he had other obligations and business demanding his attention. Even more so, the job was very political because elected officials were continually meddling in the oversight of the CCC and attempting to acquire power through their own appointees. In describing the situation Harry said, "It was tiring. It was a big job. I had camps around here in southern Idaho that kept me on the go. I was driving twenty-five thousand miles a year over these mountain roads, and I was losing sleep and losing weight. That's why I had to give it up. I had to get back to my work for the company. I'd talked it over with Jack Moon, and he was inclined to want me to stay. But I said, 'I can't do it. I've got too much to do.'"[60]

Although Harry relinquished his official title with the Corps, he remained highly involved with the program until it wound down in the Boise Basin and Valley County areas in August 1941.[61] In fact, losing the title may have allowed him even more leeway to do what he did best—work behind the scenes. Harry's continued degree of involvement post-coordinator is evident in the mandatory camp progress reports signed off on well into the 1930s. Of the three camps, McCall, Smiths Ferry, and Shafer were clearly his pet projects. If the measure of completed jobs is used as an indicator of success, Harry's

---

60   Harry C. Shellworth, interview by Elwood R. Maunder, Version #2, 53-54.

61   The program officially disbanded on June 30, 1942 at the end of the federal fiscal year, but operations ceased in most of the camps in August 1941 and more generally within Idaho in December 1941.

most prolific camps were those located at Smiths Ferry and in downtown McCall. And it is no surprise that both were located on land owned by the Boise Payette Lumber Company, and both of these camps were involved in the construction of the beautifully crafted SITPA headquarters in McCall, as well as several of the SITPA fire lookout buildings.

The Shafer Butte camp was one of his favorites, and he even featured photographs of it on Christmas cards. Revealing Harry's favoritism towards this particular camp was the consistent interchanging of the "P" and "S" designations from year-to-year indicating his creative, behind the scenes, genius of moving money to fund projects he cared most about. His vision for this camp was immense and forward-thinking. Given the relatively close proximity (fewer than twenty miles) of the Shafer Camp/Shafer Butte Lookout to the capital city of Idaho, Harry dreamed of designating nine-hundred-and-sixty acres as a municipal park to be owned and ultimately maintained by the city of Boise. Plans for the park featured running water, camp sites, and amenities for hosting events. Between 1933 and 1935 the idea gained traction and was mentioned several times in local Boise newspapers that referred to it as "Boise Mountain Park." In one of the articles, Harry said that the first time he visited the proposed park was in his early years with the lumber company in search of timber, and instead found himself struck by the sheer beauty of the area and described it as "a nature lovers' Golconda."[62]

Even years after the CCC program ended, Shellworth clung to his dream. Illustrating his sentiments, a 1945 newspaper article on the

---

62   Golconda originally referred to a ruined city located in central India. However, by the 1880s, the term was adapted to refer to a rich mine/ore deposit, or a source of great wealth.

matter states, "Shellworth was confident that in time people in high places would agree with him. When he saw the glorious view—the cathedral Sawtooths, the spectral outline of the Owyhee, the irrigated valleys and the desert below—he became, as he says, the 'Missionary of Boise Ridge.'"[63] Harry's vision never materialized. Reflecting on the situation decades later, he lamented, "I sold Senators Pope and Borah on the idea. They were all for it. But back in Washington, the Secretary of Agriculture said that if we [Boise Payette Lumber Company] would help them get that whole territory put into the Boise National Forest, they would do this work for us and the city wouldn't have any expense. That's another one of those federal promises that isn't worth a whoop in hell. They make a promise but 'none of their employees have authority to make a promise or a gentleman's agreement,' and if it gets embarrassing, that man's transferred to some other place and some other feller comes in and cannot find any record of any such agreement."[64]

---

63 "Nearby Boise Ridge Holds Rich Scenic Beauties," *The Idaho Sunday Statesman,* 14 October 1945.

64 Harry C. Shellworth, interview by Elwood R. Maunder, Version #2, 52. The site of Shellworth's Boise Mountain Park is now an undeveloped part of the Boise National Forest located north of the present day Bogus Basin ski area.

HARRY SHELLWORTH 1933.
(Johnson & Son/Shellworth Family Collection)

MCCALL, LATE 1930S LOOKING SOUTH—USFS IDAHO NATIONAL
FOREST HEADQUARTERS LEFT; MCCALL CCC CAMP LAKE
SHORE FOREGROUND, AND SITPA HEADQUARTERS, RIGHT.
(Dan LeVan Family/Holm Collection)

McCALL CCC CAMP ENTRANCE, APRIL 1940.
SITPA STATEHOUSE IN BACKGROUND.
(Walden Collection/Ivar Nelson)

4

THE STATEHOUSE
AND NEW GOLD LACE LOOKOUTS

*Perhaps the latest thing in lookouts is operated by the Southern
Idaho Timber Protective Association, of which the one on Brundage
Mountain is a fair example. Although it is 7,660 feet above the sea,
a good road runs to its door. Its glass-enclosed observation room
gleams with white paint, and its fire finder rests on a fine piece of
cabinetwork, while the plotting board swings down as needed, from
hinges. There is a neat kitchen with stove, food and dish cabinets, sink,
drainboard—everything a women could wish. The living quarters
have beds with box springs, and clothes drawers underneath.*

—STEWART HOLBROOK

Burning an Empire (1943)

With so many irons in the fire during the 1930s—the demanding job at the lumber company, SITPA, and the CCC

camps—Harry found himself spending more and more time in the field where the projects were underway. With the exception of the Shafer Butte camp, most of the activity was in Valley County between Smiths Ferry and McCall. As a result, he became very involved in the local communities, particularly McCall. In the 1930s the communities dotting Long Valley were made up of hardworking, blue-collared families that earned a living farming or working in the woods, either with a lumber company or the US Forest Service. The population in McCall from 1930 to 1940 ranged from 651 people to 875 people. The rural town was built on the south shore of Payette Lake around the local sawmill owned by the Carl Brown family. Tourism from the more populated areas of the Treasure Valley to the south, had been growing in the booming 1910s-1920s, but was greatly reduced by the hard times of the Great Depression. The southern portion of the county was economically supported by the county seat in Cascade and the railroad. It created an economic hub linking the mining districts located to the east at such places as Stibnite and, of course the timber industry. Luckier than some areas during the Great Depression, Long Valley was still grim for many who called it home.

With multiple positions, Harry had immense influence upon change and economic growth in the area. First, Boise Payette Lumber Company not only provided jobs, it also held large tracts of land, including key acreage in McCall along both sides of Lake Street between downtown and the outlet of Payette Lake, and along the North Fork of the Payette River. These lands were potentially available for future growth of the community. Second, SITPA was another avenue of employment for locals and could move private and state funds into rural areas. Third, the funding available through the CCC enabled administrators to funnel federal money into rural areas to build lasting infrastructure and at the same time provide jobs.

Harry and other administrators of the CCC recognized from the beginning that the program was not a long-term economic fix, but rather a short-term stimulus to help create an infrastructure and spur industry that in return would perpetuate economic growth in the future. In the case of Harry's camps, the infrastructure and industry came in the form of roads, bridges, trails, and buildings, and thus yielded one of Harry's most visible and lasting legacies to the state of Idaho. The work of the McCall camp, like others, contributed to fire control efforts and general forest management tasks of the day, but more importantly it also greatly contributed to a budding tourist industry in McCall, with several prime examples still in use. The CCC boys from this camp built the road around Payette Lake, extensively rebuilt the historic Warren Wagon Road from McCall over Secesh Summit to Burgdorf and onto Warren,[65] helped to construct portions of the road extending up Lake Fork Creek toward Lick Creek

---

65   For more information on the cultural significance of the Warren Wagon Road see: Jerry Wylie. *Cultural Resource Inventory of the Warren Wagon Road Idaho and Valley Counties, Idaho, Payette National Forest.* McCall, ID: Payette National Forest, 1981. In reference to the road he states, "[T]he State Wagon Road undoubtedly contributed to the economic and cultural development of this part of the state. As such it represents the development of state and local transportation systems ca. 1891-1930. (Because of extensive reconstruction by CCC crews, the original road effectively ceased to exist after the 1930's.) However, since it was completed after Warren's mining boom it contributed little to the exploitation of the region mineral wealth. During the Thunder Mountain rush at the turn of the century it was only one of several routes to the mines in use at that time. The Wagon Road was not directly associated with the Warren mining boom and was not originally connected to that community. In fact, the name 'Warren Wagon Road' in common usage today is a misnomer; it was never called that originally. 'Territorial Wagon Road,' 'Salmon River Wagon Road,' State Wagon Road,' or simply 'wagon road' were the names used in the literature and on maps dating from the period 1889 –1912."

Summit, built the Little Ski Hill,[66] established a fish hatchery facility in McCall, and greatly improved what is now Ponderosa State Park.[67] All of these pieces and parts solidified year-round recreation and tourism in the community. Much of the success of the CCC program can be attributed to the good leadership and innovations brought about by such people as Harry.

Symbiotic relationships formed with Harry orchestrating the funds readily available through the New Deal programs, the CCC, and the power of the lumber company. The private industry, the public, and economic welfare of the area all benefited. In need of centrally locating CCC camps and modernizing the SITPA facilities, Harry arranged for the Boise Payette Lumber Company to lease land to the CCCs for the main McCall camp, as well as donate land to SITPA for a new site in McCall, both of which were centrally located

---

66 For more information on the history of the Little Ski Hill see: Margaret Fuller, Doug Fuller, and Jerry Painter. *Ski the Great Potato: Idaho Ski Areas Past and Present.* Weiser, ID: Trail Guide Books, 2013. 93-98. The CCC constructed a log lodge and brushed out the primary ski runs. The famous wooden ski jump was built shortly after World War II and the CCC lodge burned down in 1954 and was replaced with a modern building in 1956.Based on Valley County Courthouse records and an interview with Earl Dodds (18 December 2020) the Little Ski Hill land was initially owned by the Boise Payette Lumber Company. Carl Brown's son, Warren, had a great interest in developing downhill skiing in the area. Presumably the Browns worked with Harry to purchase the land for the ski hill. Subsequently, the Browns then transferred the ownership of the land to the US Forest Service and a lease between the ski hill organization and the government was established.

67 Based on correspondence between the author and Rick Just, an authority on Idaho State Parks, Ponderosa State Park did not become designated a state park until 1957 when the Idaho State Land Board began calling it a state park. Even then, the Land Board referenced "creating" Ponderosa State Park as recently as 1966, just when the Idaho Department was getting organized. According to Rick Just the actually creation is a "slippery issue" as confusion about when certain sites became state parks is mostly due to the loose use of the term from the beginning of the twentieth century to present. In the early years any state land where one could throw down a picnic blanket was sometimes called a state park. There are several references, even as early as 1911; to the peninsula on Payette Lake being a state park, but it would be most accurate to identify it simply as state land prior to 1957.

downtown. The SITPA site was strategically positioned adjacent to the Forest Service's main compound; the CCC headquarters was situated a stone's throw across Lake Street on the shores of Payette Lake. The three properties blended into a distinct, cohesive campus canopied by tall ponderosa pines and open views to the north of the lake and to the granite ridges of the West Central Mountains. The combined sites symbolized the renewed economic prosperity of the area, and at the time occupied a major portion of the town. They were utilitarian because they were designed to house large groups of men, equipment, and serve as a base of operations. Predictably, based on the development of Harry's Gold Lace Lookouts, the SITPA campus in McCall outshined them all.

Anticipating future tourism growth in northern Valley County, and thus the potential of increased man-caused fire activity, the Association moved its primary headquarters to McCall, and the Smiths Ferry administrative site became secondary. Still, CCC labor and money were used to improve and expand operations at Smiths Ferry during this period. Construction on the McCall facility began in 1936 and continued through 1940. When finished, it consisted of eight permanent buildings, five of which reflected the utilitarian needs of the Association and were board and batten construction and included a machine shop, storage facilities, and garages.[68] However, the three most visible buildings on the five-acre site were situated at the southeast corner of State and Lake streets. These improvements were handcrafted of native logs built to showcase local workman-ship—they included the Statehouse, garage/bunkhouse, and pump

---

68   Southern Idaho Timber Protective Association Annual Reports from 1936 to 1941 on file at the SITPA Office, McCall, ID.

house. Living in the new residence was a perk of the fire warden position.[69] Chief Fire Warden Bill Campbell, who had been with the Association for a number of years at Smiths Ferry and prior to that as a fire patrolman, was the first to occupy the grand building. He and his wife Lucile lived in the house until the spring of 1944.

The Statehouse or Fire Warden's House, as it is commonly called today, is a deceptively large residential dwelling, two-and-one-half-stories tall with a full basement. Construction began in 1936 and was finished the following year. The home was designed for entertaining, and with a half dozen bedrooms to accommodate overnighters. The house has a number of unique features, including an office with a slate fireplace, a large open dining area, and two-and-one-half baths. Constructed using simple but elegant architecture, it features beautiful Finnish log work with full-dovetailed corners, because Harry again employed John Heikkila and Gust Lapinoja as the foremen. Also on the Finnish carpentry crew were Martin Heikkila and Reino Kantola.

The interior design of the Statehouse is as stunning as the exterior, and extra care was taken to highlight the many native tree species. As a result, nothing on the interior is painted or covered. The only wood to be imported from outside Idaho is oak flooring used in the living room, the dining room, and the glass-enclosed front porch. Everything is wood: floors, walls, ceilings, picture frames, curtain rods, and even the curtain rod rings. All of the furnishings in the house were custom built to fit the theme, including the flower vases,

---

69 The only building on the site featuring the high quality of construction associated with the Finnish men is the Statehouse. It is speculated that Heikkila and Lapinoja may have overseen the construction of the other buildings from 1937 through 1940, but according to Finnish construction expert Frank Eld, the buildings are not indicative of their work.

candlesticks, and stands to hold ashtrays. The upstairs rooms have built-in beds constructed like ship berths with drawers below, a design no doubt influenced by Harry's days in the sea transport service.

A sister improvement to the Statehouse was also constructed by the CCC in Boise in 1940. Chateau de Bois, or "The Cabin" as it is known as today, featured many of the same architectural elements and was constructed to honor the fiftieth anniversary of Idaho's statehood, as well as house the State Forestry Department and the Soil Conservation Corp.[70] Similar to the Statehouse, it featured Idaho native wood. The general labor for the project was provided by the state's McConnel CCC camp based in Boise. The skilled laborers were employed with the help of Harry, and he again brought on John Heikkila and Lapinoja as foremen.[71] Other Finnish axmen working on the job were Reino Kantola and Martin Heikkila.[72] State Forester Franklin Girard acknowledged the craftsmanship in his dedication brochure for the house: "The log work on the building was done by two expert Finlander round log artists, loaned to the state of Idaho by that true conservation agency, the Southern Idaho Timber Protective Association, which has employed the Finns in the construction of lookout towers and lookout houses for the Association for a number of years."[73] The grounds around the building were landscaped with

---

70 This property was occupied by the State Forestry Department and the Soil Conservation Corp until 1990. The city of Boise acquired ownership in 1992. Most recently the building has been used as a literary center known as The Cabin: A Center for Readers & Writers.

71 Franklin Girard. *Chateau de Bois: Idaho Cooperative Board of Forestry.* May 1940, 3. Holm Collection.

72 Allan Maki and Bernice Heikkila Hendrix, relatives of John and Martin Heikkila, Personal Communication, 26 May 2020.

73 Franklin Girard. *Chateau de Bois: Idaho Cooperative Board of Forestry.* May 1940, 3. Holm Collection.

all native plants including sumac, syringe, aspen, wild honeysuckle, and wild rose.

The SITPA compound in McCall was used for official business, as well as being Harry's unofficial second home for entertaining friends and influencing important guests. He frequented it so often that the bedroom at the southwest corner of the second floor became his room. Harry fostered close relationships with the SITPA fire wardens and their families and one of the benefits was living in the Statehouse. Following the Campbells was the Art Roberts family—the longest tenants from the spring of 1944 to 1966. A principal purpose of the house was to host and board people related to SITPA business. The Roberts humorously called it "a bed-and-breakfast without the break-fast." Throughout all four seasons guests came and went, and generally returned more than once. Many close friendships ensued. Of all the people to visit and stay at the house, Harry was the favorite of the Roberts. Art and his wife Doris had two young girls, Josephine "Jo" and Patsy "Pat." The two kids instantly took to Harry, who became the grandfather they never had.

The Roberts girls first met him in the summer of 1944. Jo, the older of the two by eleven months, still remembers it well, "This wonderful jolly man came into the living room where Patsy and I were playing on the floor. He was carrying two huge stuffed toy bears…I was four at the time—he said in a booming voice, 'Now, who do we have here?' I squeaked out, 'I'm Jo and this is Patsy.' I had red hair and Patsy had ash blonde hair which, I think, prompted Harry to give us our nicknames, which we would have as long as we knew him. He said to me as he tossed the larger of the two bears to me, 'You're Rusty!' Then tossing the black and white panda to Patsy, he said, 'And you're Dusty.' Whenever he came to McCall, he brought us more wonders."[74] Harry gave the girls their first bubble gum, their first balloon (nonexistent owing to rubber shortage during World War II), and as they aged gave them camping equipment. Even more treasured than any item Harry ever gave them on his visits was his time. "He let us crawl all over him. He had the most wonderful pipe-tobacco smell about him…He used to walk 'uptown' with us to the drug store where he would buy us strawberry ice cream sodas." Ironically, neither of the girls cared for the sodas, but it did not matter since they were with Harry. In the summer Harry frequently took them huckleberry picking. "After one of those huckleberry mornings, he took Patsy and me to the newly opened Shore Lodge for breakfast. I remember our mother was horrified that he had taken the two of us dirty huckleberry-stained rag-tags to the beautiful Shore Lodge. Harry just laughed and told her what a good time we had."[75]

According to Jo and Pat, Harry thought every child should have a pet, and he insisted on giving them a dog. Without giving Art and Doris much choice, Harry bought the girls a brown and white cocker spaniel named Sandy. After a car killed Sandy, Harry gave the girls another cocker—a beautiful blonde male. Since the dog joined their family during Christmas, they named him "Nicky" in honor of Saint Nicholas. When the two girls thought Harry could do no wrong, however, he called Doris one winter day to say that he was bringing a big treat, "To our little six-year-old horror, that 'treat' was his granddaughter Sandy! We had been replaced! Actually, our memories of Sandy are that she was a sweet little girl."[76]

---

74 Jo (Roberts) Peterson. Letter to Richard Holm, Jr. 24 January 2020.

75 Jo (Roberts) Peterson. Letter to Richard Holm, Jr. 24 January 2020.

76 Jo (Roberts) Peterson. Letter to Richard Holm, Jr. 24 January 2020.

In addition to the SITPA headquarters in McCall and Smiths Ferry, the CCC program provided the labor and money for the construction of a completely new lookout at No Business (1936-1937) and the replacement of lookout buildings at Brundage Mountain (1937-1938) and Packer John (1935-1936).[77] These three facilities are arguably some of the finer fire lookouts ever constructed. Built on the similar two-story design employed at Shafer Butte in the late 1920s, Harry's second generation of Gold Lace Lookouts enlarged the actual structures two feet in each direction to 20' x 20'. He also incorporated large exterior wraparound concrete and stone observation decks along the main floor. To facilitate public access and the moving of equipment, exterior stairs were nearly all eliminated and, instead, broad concrete ramps provided access to the viewing areas and the main entrances. The walkways and observation decks were lined with large hand-hewn timbers for railings. The intentional use of native material tended to blend the design and draw the architecture of the building into the natural surroundings. Most notably, these three lookouts of the CCC-era, compared to the earlier lookouts constructed by the Association had a much higher level of finish carpentry and were generally of higher quality-work than most homes built at the time. The foremen on these three lookouts were again Heikkila and Lapinoja. Matching outhouses, also featuring the highly skilled craftsmanship, adorned the lookout locations.

Proud of all of his Gold Lace Lookouts, Harry not only wanted them to be functional, equipped with the best instruments of the time,

---

77   Southern Idaho Timber Protective Association Annual Reports from 1936 to 1941 on file at the SITPA Office, McCall, ID. Also referenced: "*The Idaho Daily Statesman's* Monday Picture Page [featuring Packer John Lookout]," *Idaho Statesman*, 19 October 1936.

and distinctive in design, he also wanted them to be uniquely recognizable by name. When SITPA selected the site for the Association's new lookout facility to be installed at what is now called No Business, the name for the prominent knob on official maps was Bally Mountain or Bald Mountain. Harry told a reporter for *The Idaho Statesman* the name would not do—there were already too many peaks and mountains in the state with those names and "his" new lookout might be confused. Harry turned to history for ideas and interviewed a Weiser sheep man, who years earlier had kept a summer camp at the location of the proposed lookout. The man hired as the sheepherder to run the camp returned to headquarters after a few days on the job. He recounted how a troublesome bear had scattered the sheep and caused mayhem, telling his boss, "A sheepherder has no business on that mountain." Harry cherished the story and renamed the prominent knob.[78]

As with the first generation of Gold Lace Lookouts, it was important to Harry to have a fine collection of photographs for publicity. Old friend Ansgar Johnson, Sr. again was hired to photograph the new lookouts, as well as the new administrative site in McCall. Kenneth D. "K.D." Swan, another photographer Harry crossed paths with in photographing his first generation of lookouts, also photographed CCC operations. Swan was perhaps more regionally well-known than Johnson, but both had an eye for black and white landscape photography. Swan lived in Missoula, Montana, and was an employee of the US Forest Service from 1911 to 1947. He graduated from Harvard University with a master's degree in forestry and moved west. After

---

78 "Fleeing Sheepherder Gives Name to New Idaho Lookout," *The Idaho Sunday Statesman*, 15 November 1936.

two years with the agency on several forests, he was assigned to the Northern Region, where he first worked as a draftsman. K.D. had a keen interest in photography as a hobby, which in the early 1920s led him to be assigned to the Information and Education Branch. One of his primary jobs was to travel the region (Montana, Idaho, and the Dakotas) capturing the beauty of the landscapes and the activities of the agency.

The images were widely used in US Forest Service publications, but were used by K.D. for public presentations and educational programs for the general public and school children as well. When Harry organized trips with high-ranking forestry officials, including representatives from the US Forest Service, Swan sometimes tagged along as the designated photographer. K.D. was meticulous in setting up his shots. He was very conscientious about not wasting film and getting just the right composition: angle, view, light, and subject. It was not uncommon for one image to take him hours to arrange.[79] His landscape work is comparable in light and composition to that of Ansel Adams. Some of the best images of the first generation of the Gold Lace Lookouts were captured by Swan; probably the most interesting are those of the Brundage Mountain Lookout at night with lanterns lighting the interior. As for the 1930s photographs, K.D. took a great interest in the CCC. His most noteworthy images of this era, where

---

79 Kenneth D. Swan. *Splendid Was the Trail*. Missoula, MT: Mountain Press, 1968. This autobiographical account is the most exhaustive source on the career and work of K.D. Swan. Well-known western writer Norman Maclean credits Swan as a major influence in his writing career on the art and understanding of composition. The two met when Maclean was a youngster in the Boy Scout troop led by K.D. Swan. Then as a teenager Maclean worked one summer as his assistant on US Forest Service photographic expeditions. For more on this see: Ron McFarland and Hugh Nichols (editors). *Norman Maclean: American Authors Series*. (Lewiston, ID: Confluence Press, Inc., 1988). 100-12.

he and Harry overlapped professionally, were related to the CCC camps in the McCall area.

STATEHOUSE MCCALL SITPA COMPOUND RECENTLY COMPLETED.
(Johnson & Son/Jim & Lucile Campbell/Eve Brassey Chandler Collection)

SITPA CHIEF FIRE WARDEN JIM CAMPBELL
AND HARRY STATEHOUSE STEPS 1940.
(Johnson & Son/Jim & Lucile Campbell/Eve Brassey Chandler Collection)

HARRY AND JOHNNY HARGRAVE STATEHOUSE 1930S.
(Shellworth Family Collection)

STATEHOUSE LIVING ROOM 1930S.
(Johnson & Son/Jim & Lucile Campbell/Eve Brassey Chandler Collection)

STATEHOUSE LIVING ROOM AND DINING ROOM 1930S.
(Johnson & Son /Jim & Lucile Campbell/Eve Brassey Chandler Collection)

STATEHOUSE GLASS-ENCLOSED FRONT PORCH
1930S. HARRY IN BACKGROUND.
(Johnson & Son/Jim & Lucile Campbell/Eve Brassey Chandler Collection)

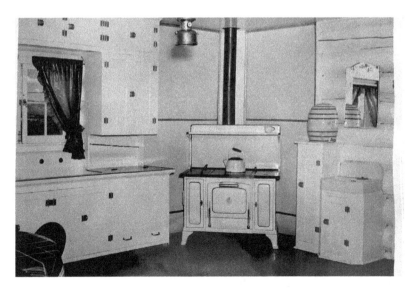

MAIN FLOOR BRUNDAGE MOUNTAIN LOOKOUT 1930S – "GOLD LACE!"
(Johnson & Son/SITPA Collection)

JO AND PATSY ROBERTS AT THE SITPA HEADQUARTERS
1947 WITH DOG NICKY, A GIFT FROM HARRY.
(Roberts Family Collection/Pat Benninghoff/Jo Peterson)

CCC-BUILT BRUNDAGE MOUNTAIN LOOKOUT, 1930S. HARRY'S
FAVORITE DOUBLE WHITEBARK PINES IN THE FOREGROUND.
(Johnson & Son/SITPA Collection)

CCC-BUILT NO BUSINESS LOOKOUT ALMOST COMPLETE.
(Johnson & Son/SITPA Collection)

MCCALL CCC CAMP BEACH DURING CCC WATER CARNIVAL
1930S. BROWN FAMILY SAWMILL IN BACKGROUND. K.D.
SWAN DOCUMENTARY PHOTOGRAPH OF CCC LIFE.
(K.D. Swan/USFS/Ivar Nelson)

5

HARRY'S DREAMLAND— THE IDAHO PRIMITIVE AREA

The Middle Fork of the Salmon River in the Primitive Area is accessible by pack trip from strategic points on the loop or the remotest reaches of the Thunder Mountain region and the last zeniths of Chamberlain Basin. The topography in general is of rugged mountainous landscape, heavily blanketed with forests, laced with thousands of streams, broken open by canyons more than a mile in depth, and topped by summits that stand two miles above the sea. The wind moves gently here, or falls into a skyful of lazy breezes, each burgeoned with the fragrance of wild flowers and evergreens and a clean sky.
—VARDIS FISHER
Idaho Guide (1937)

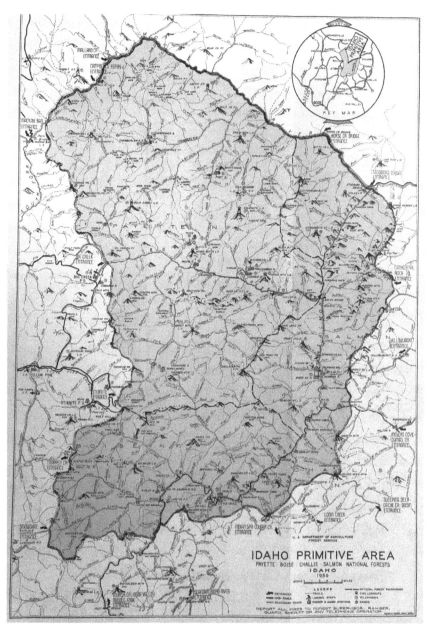

EXPANDED IDAHO PRIMITIVE AREA BOUNDARIES.
(USFS Payette NF Heritage Program Collection)

When not busy with his family, work, or volunteer efforts on numerous boards, Shellworth could be found planning his next outdoor leisure trip. While he took frequent trips to hunt and fish, for relaxation he took an annual month-long sabbatical deep into the Idaho mountains. By the early 1920s his destination for these adventures was the largest unpopulated area in the central part of the state—the Salmon River Mountains. And, at the heart of this rugged country, was likely his favorite place—the Big Creek drainage, which is one of the main tributaries to the Middle Fork of the Salmon River. Harry treasured the isolated country so much that he labeled his personal files on the subject, "My Dreamland." A multi-decade love affair developed with this region and likely remains as Harry's greatest contribution to Idaho—the establishment of the Idaho Primitive Area.

Harry's adventures in the Big Creek area varied, depending on the season. He hunted, fished, or simply took in the beauty. He explored many different places by using diverse trailheads, such as Seafoam, the Big Horn Crags, Thunder Mountain, and Edwardsburg, among others. However, there were two constants: a visit to the Big Creek drainage and horseback transportation. From the nearest road he enjoyed leaving the mechanized world behind. Harry had picked up riding skills from his father but did not own his own stock and pack equipment; therefore he hired professional outfitters whom he had become well acquainted with over the years. Some of the outfitters he used were Bill Moore, Guy Fisher, Claude Gillespie, Tom Williams, Clarke Cox, Sam Cupp, and Blackie Wallace. Although a good number of trips were for leisure, Harry more commonly linked some aspect of business with the trip, and thus he invited friends with whom he had business or political relations. The trips were not just for men;

women and children as well, and the trips were not just shared with locals from Idaho—more often Easterners whom he had met during his dealings in Washington, D.C. These ranged from members of the Weyerhaeuser family, to judges, lumber company owners, foresters, politicians, and general outdoor enthusiasts. Among certain circles of friends, especially in the East, Harry's pack trip forays became legendary and in many ways helped to define him—a gregarious Westerner. As evident in his personal papers, Harry was consulted for decades about the details of camping, hunting, and fishing in the remote central area of Idaho. Not uncommonly many planned trips never materialized. On many occasions he invited prominent figures who never carved out the necessary time to travel to Idaho and be gone for weeks. Most notable among these was a planned trip with Herbert Hoover in 1927 when he was Secretary of Commerce.[80]

Harry's passion for the area and pure enjoyment of planning the trips is apparent in this December 1930 letter to friend J. O. Stewart of Brooklyn, New York: "*I can recall most vividly, on such a day as this, each detail of this trail from where it leaves the high mountain meadow, thru forest, "burn", and glade down to the canyons of the clear noisy rivers, thru slide rock, over pine bench lands and thru gorges, castellated and cathedral-like, past lily pad lakes, over wave-like mountain tops with here and there a "hill-billy" friend to climax the evenings camp, and gentle deer to punctuate interest in the day's trip, and I see, again, the lazy drift of the camp fire's smoke over a dainty, mountain encompassed, lakelet [sic]… The rose heather near the ridges, the purple and green of the creeping Juniper alongside the trail, the regal Bear Grass Lily showing thru wooded*

80   William E. Borah. Letter to Harry C. Shellworth. 13 September 1927. Shellworth Family Collection.

aisles, the graceful columbine along the creeks and blue penstemon on the hillside, wood violets in the meadows, are all tucked in several feet of white waiting for the touch of spring and in the deep snow there is no sign of life save the trail of beaver and otter along the streams and mink and marten in the white robed forest and next summer is, in time, eons away, in the future, and above all other curses I hate waiting."[81]

Harry had the innate ability to make a trip a once-in-a-lifetime experience. His skills as an outdoorsman, as well as his in-depth knowledge of the flora and fauna, made the trip unique. The terrain and scenery spoke for themselves. But what really set a Shellworth trip apart was his personality and connections. Along the way, Harry knew everyone and everyone knew Harry. He was pals with the owners of the dude ranches, the working ranchers, the Forest Service personnel at the ranger stations, the owners of the remote mining operations, and best of all he was pals with eccentric backcountry characters who inhabited the remote lands year-round: "Cougar" Dave Lewis, William Allen "Stoney" Stonebraker, the Elliott brothers, "Profile" Sam Willson, and the Edwards family of Edwardsburg.

Often Harry would have a person on the trip that had never spent a night in the outdoors. To put them at ease he developed an ice-breaker by sending in advance or handing out to each guest a wallet-sized leather pouch labeled "Deposit Slips," for the safe keeping of toilet paper (a luxury while camping). The title of slips varied. Most common was "Idaho Primitive Area Deposit Slips." For a personal

81 Harry C. Shellworth. Letter to Mr. J.O. Stewart, 4 December 1930. Harry C. Shellworth Collection MS-269, Idaho State Historical Society Archives. Stewart and his son joined Harry on a pack trip through the Idaho Primitive Area in 1930. Based on letters of correspondence between the men found in the Idaho State Historical Society Archives the two were good friends. Stewart owned the Stewart Lumber Company located in Brooklyn, New York.

touch, below the label the individual's name was etched, followed by "Depositor." The joke played out well in his favor—either in bemused responses by mail before the trip, or lots of banter upon greeting the individual or party at the start. Harry thought so highly of his deposit slip invention that, with the help of attorneys, he explored the idea of patenting the dispenser and trademarking "Idaho Primitive Area Deposit Slips." It appears he saved most, if not all, of the thank-you responses in his personal correspondence files, numbering nearly one-hundred letters.

Even after Harry's annual pack trips waned in the late 1930s, he continued to send them out in gratitude to people for nearly another decade. The deposit slips in many ways became a symbol of being a member of Harry's inner circle. Harry sometimes gave honorary memberships to what he called the "Idaho Primitive Area Association" via the deposit-slip holders. An extrovert, he even extended an invitation in May 1937 to President Franklin D. Roosevelt via a mutual friend, Nelson C. Brown, who was the state forester of New York and head of the Department of Forest Utilization at the New York State College of Forestry at Syracuse University.[82] Whether or not Roosevelt accepted is unknown, but Brown wrote back. "I expect to see him [Roosevelt] at his summer home at Hyde Park on the Hudson this summer, perhaps in June, and will present him the certificate at that time. I feel that he would

---

82 Attached to the Nelson C. Brown's thank-you letter dated 29 May 1937 in the Shellworth Family Collection, Harry included a handwritten note stating, "When I was handling CCC camps in Idaho, under special authority for Governor C. Ben Ross the political jackals got after me because I selected camp supervisors etc. from my knowledge of their efficiency—paying very scant attention to political preference lists. Nelson C. Brown, was sent out to Idaho to investigate me. He gave me complete vindication and full approval of all my acts & 'vision and efficiency.'"

understand and appreciate this certificate very much more if tendered to him in person…As you probably know, the President does not walk about so that it would be difficult for him to use this certificate in the woods. He has had Infantile Paralysis which means that he must be lifted in and out of every automobile and train. This fact is not generally known and you will recall that no photograph is ever taken showing him in this condition. This is a courtesy extended to him as President…The President has a keen sense of humor and gets a great kick out of every funny situation that arises."[83]

Besides his outgoing personality, Harry, as mentioned, befriended the few remaining year-round residents in the depths of the rugged Salmon River Mountains who made a meager living off the land by guiding hunting trips, trapping, and mining. Chief among them were Dave Lewis on the lower end of the Big Creek canyon, and above the drainage to north in the expansive Chamberlain Basin William Allen "Stoney" Stonebraker. The latter had settled in the country during the days of the Thunder Mountain Gold Rush when the country was teeming with miners. Lewis settled shortly thereafter. As people fled the area in the wake of the busted economy, a few held on, surviving the economic shift by converting to tourism, trapping, or subsistence living. From the beginning of Harry's early trips, these characters became integral to his guests having a good time. In essence, he was able to share with them these very special friendships because he recognized they were part of the landscape and instrumental to understanding the land. In some cases his introduction facilitated friendships of their own.

---

83 Nelson C. Brown. Letter to Harry C. Shellworth. 29 May 1937. Shellworth Family Collection.

The economic shift from mining to tourism had its consequences. To old-school sportsman, who preferred being part of the horse-and-mule class, the increasing use of aircraft was seen as nothing less than an intrusion into their remote and relatively private paradise. Increasingly concerned about the future of the land surrounding the Big Creek environs, Harry and his comrades began exploring avenues of preservation. A common thread in his correspondence during this time was exploring a legal avenue to protect the land with restrictive laws on what could be done there—a game preserve. One can speculate that the major catalyst for the preservation of this remote area of the Salmon River Mountains was the ever-increasing use of aircraft to access it for fire suppression efforts by the US Forest Service, and by sportsman for fishing and big-game hunting. By the mid-1920s the airplane was no longer a novelty. Instead, it was considered a somewhat safe and legitimate mode of transportation. For an old-fashioned horse-and-mule man such as Shellworth, the airplane was doubtless threat to his personal retreat—instead of a several-day pack trip to reach Big Creek; it could be done by airplane within an hour from the nearest town.

Harry was not the only one in opposition to the invasion of aircraft; many other outdoorsmen thought the new access to be un-sportsman like. Those in favor, however, were the owners of the remote in-holdings who were trying to make a living outfitting as a means of hanging on to their homesteads and way of life. After all, it was the most efficient means to transport clients in and out of the backcountry. In fact, one of Harry's closest backcountry friends, Stony, was at the forefront of promoting aviation in the backcountry, since the meadow adjacent to his house was where the first aircraft landing was made in the region (c. 1925). Eventually, more than half the owners of homesteads along the roadless river corridors built runways. Another early example was Merl "Blackie" Wallace's at the Flying W Ranch on Cabin Creek (1931). In Big Creek proper the Forest Service built two early airstrips—one at the Big Creek administrative site (1929) and the other at Soldier Bar (1933), both in the defense of and need of fire suppression, but they were also opened for public use.

For years, Harry, and his friends who joined him on the annual pack trips, talked of ways to limit and prevent future intrusions and further development in the Big Creek area and the broader region of the roadless areas in the Salmon River Mountains. By the early-to mid-1920s, game preserves were established in the area of the Middle Fork of the Salmon River to protect wildlife, primarily along the river corridors. Several reserves were combined in 1925 under the title of the Middle Fork Preserve.[84] Then by the mid to-late 1920s, the idea of wilderness areas as we know them began to circulate among wildlife managers, foresters, and politicians. Although the federal designation of "wilderness" would not evolve for nearly another thirty years, the term the Forest Service used then was "primitive area."

Two events fell into place for Harry to meet his goal of preserving the area. First, in 1927 he pulled together a remarkable group of people for his annual trip. The group consisted of Idaho Governor Clarence Baldridge, Intermountain District Forester Richard H. Rutledge, professional photographer Ansgar Johnson, Sr., Boise lawyer Jess Hawley, mining executive Stanley Easton, and forester Andy

---

84 Ken Robison. *Defending Idaho's Natural Heritage*. Boise, ID: Self-published, 2014. 89.

Casner.[85] This group also shared Harry's vision, and, according to Shellworth, brought "new life and impetus" to the movement. Second, in July 1929 the Forest Service established a legal platform under the L-20 Regulations to establish such a federally protected area.[86] With political back-channeling handled by Harry, several key figures at the state level (Governor Baldridge) and federal level (Senator Borah and Intermountain District Forester Richard H. Rutledge) joined together in cohesive support of preserving the triangular area between the Middle Fork of the Salmon River, South Fork of the Salmon River, and the main Salmon River, using the new "primitive area" designation. A draft proposal was developed by the Forest Service detailing the area to be preserved and it was sent to Governor Baldridge in November 1930.

Under the direction of Baldridge, a committee was formed regarding the proposed primitive area, and strategically he appointed Harry

---

85 Richard "Dick" H. Rutledge started with the US Forest Service in September 1905. He rose through the ranks of the agency serving as a regional forester by the end of the 1920s and ended his career with a post in Washington, D.C., where he often served as an advisor to Interior Secretary Harold Ickes. After suffering a nervous breakdown he retired from the Forest Service in 1944. His heart always remained in the West, as he helped his parents homestead in Long Valley, Idaho, near Roseberry in 1888. When he retired, Rutledge and his wife Mary (Pottenger), settled first in Boise until 1952, and then eventually to Billings, Montana, to be near one of their daughters. He died in November 1956, and is buried in Sunset Memorial Gardens cemetery. Rutledge and Harry had a lifelong friendship. The relationship was paramount to the success of the Idaho Primitive Area designation and the establishment of the CCC in Idaho.

86 Definition of "L-20 Regulation" from "Briefing on Primitive Areas in the National Forest System," Statement of M. Rupert Cutler, Assistant Secretary for Conservation, Research, and Education, U. S. Department of Agriculture, Before Subcommittee on Public Lands of the Committee on Interior and Insular Affairs, U.S. House of Representatives, July 24, 1979. "The L-20 Regulation provided a policy to designate Natural Areas, for scientific and educational purposes; Experimental Forests and Ranges, for long-term research unfettered by other management objectives; and Primitive Areas 'to maintain primitive conditions of transportation, subsistence, habitation, and environment to the fullest degree compatible with their highest public use.'"

as chairman. The committee consisted of eleven men, primarily
Republicans with political backgrounds, and representatives of major
natural resource industries (farmers, stockman, a wool-grower, a game
warden, mining operator, etc.). Shellworth and Baldridge covered their
bases with the men they selected who could gather further support for
the idea. For example, the upper reaches of Big Creek held important
mineral deposits in the Thunder Mountain area and Harry knew he
needed the support of miners—after all, while the L-20 Regulations had
stringent land use restrictions, not all industrial uses such as mining
and grazing were forbidden. Primitive areas were defined by the L-20
Regulations as, "To prevent the unnecessary elimination or impairment
of unique natural values, and to conserve, so far as controlling economic
consideration will permit, the opportunity to the public to oversee the
conditions which existed in the pioneer phases of the Nation's development, and to engage in the forms of outdoor recreation characteristic of
that period; thus aiding to preserve national traditions, ideals, and characteristic, and promoting a truer understanding of historical phases
of national progress."[87] With widespread support from key people, the
US Forest Service created the 1,087,744 acre Idaho Primitive Area in
March 1931 (later increased to 1,232,744 acres).[88] Decades later, Harry

---

87 Gerald W. Williams. *The Forest Service: Fighting for Public Lands.* Westport, CT: Greenwood
Press, 2007. 177-78.

88 Dennis and Lynn Baird's scholarly article "A Campfire Vision: Establishing the Idaho Primitive
Area" published in the *Journal of the West* (July 1987) is the definitive source of the creation of the Idaho Primitive Area. The piece includes an excellent list of references, including primary sources and information taken from an interview the Bairds conducted with
Eugene Shellworth (Harry's son) in December 1984. Dennis Baird is a wilderness advocate
who served as an early member of Ted Trueblood's River of No Return Wilderness Council
and retired from the University of Idaho after forty some years of service with the title of
Librarian Emeritus with rank of Professor. His wife Lynn also retired from a long career with
the University of Idaho Library.

would write next to his signature line on his "last copy" of the typed transcript from the December 20, 1930, Governor's Meeting on the Proposed Primitive Area, "Result = No statutory action by Congress, multiple use Forest Service, State Civil & criminal law, fish & game laws only, entirely satisfactory to Idaho. To Hell with Federalism."[89]

In the years to follow more remote areas of Idaho were designated "primitive"– the Selway-Bitterroot Primitive Area (1,239,840 acres), the Salmon River Breaks Primitive Area (216,870 acres), and the Sawtooth Primitive Area (200,940 acres). In 1939 the Forest Service's L-20 Regulation gave way to the more restrictive U Regulations. The U Regulations were significant as the term "wilderness" replaced "primitive" and remained in place until the passage of the federal Wilderness Act in 1964. Then in 1973, Idaho native and well-known outdoor writer Ted Trueblood, began a grass-roots campaign, similar to Harry's efforts in the 1920s, to establish the Idaho Primitive Area, along with other adjacent lands, as a federally designated wilderness area. He teamed up with US Senator Frank Church of Idaho, who had sponsored the Wilderness Act, and in 1980 pushed the Central Idaho Wilderness Act into law, establishing the 2.3 million acres of land designated as the River of No Return Wilderness Area.[90] Shellworth's original

---

89 Copy of the typed transcript from the Governor's Committee on the Proposed Primitive Area, Harry C. Shellworth Collection MS-269, Idaho State Historical Society Archives.

90 The Ted Trueblood Papers are housed at the Boise State University Library in the Special Collections and Archives (MSS 089). The archives include extensive information on the establishment of the River of No Return Wilderness, as well as the formation and efforts of the River of No Return Wilderness Council founded by Trueblood. Also at the Boise State University Library in the Special Collections and Archives are the Frank Church Papers (MSS 56), which encompass further information on the subject. The River of No Return Wilderness Council Records, 1973-1979 (MG 452), are housed at the University of Idaho Library in the Special Collections and Archives.

primitive area, concentrated on the Middle Fork of the Salmon River, was at the center of the massive federally-protected area. Today it is the second-largest wilderness area in the lower forty-eight states, only outsized by the noncontiguous Death Valley Wilderness (3.1 million acres). Congress renamed the area the "Frank Church River of No Return Wilderness" in 1984 to honor Church, who recently had died.

Although the Idaho Primitive Area can largely be considered Harry's greatest contribution to Idaho and to the current wilderness preservation system, it did not come to fruition without compromises. After all, Harry was a land agent for a major lumber company—the bottom line of his job was to buy land with large stands of timber for the production of lumber. However, according to his family, Harry was a firm proponent of multiple-use concepts long before they were a popular idea. In essence, he thought there should be land held privately and publicly for the specific uses of timber and mineral extraction under ethical practices, and that there also should be land specifically set aside purely for preservation. It is also quite plausible, given Harry's background and knowledge of the timber industry, that he well recognized that the land within the designated Idaho Primitive Area held limited stands of merchantable timber owing to low-tree densities, slow growth, and the high cost of remote extraction.

While Harry and his committee were able to compromise with supporters and opponents over the timber, mining, and grazing issues surrounding the creation of the Idaho Primitive Area, two issues went unresolved and decades later loomed large. The first was the federal government's intent to purchase the private inholdings, when they came up for sale, many of which were occupied by Harry's friends.[91] The second was allowing designated landing fields for aircraft. Neither issue was widely discussed publically by Harry, but small hints can be found in his daily correspondence with his friends and acquaintances. After William Allen Stonebraker died unexpectedly in 1932, his widow, Golda, contacted Harry hoping he could help sell the ranch in Chamberlain Basin. Based on his letters Harry clearly favored government acquisitions of private inholdings. For example in a letter to J.O. Stewart in October 1932 Harry wrote, "Twice during the past year I have had prospective buyers [for the ranch] but both times failed to complete a sale, once because of bank failure and the other on account of a change of plans by the prospective buyer. The Idaho Primitive Area has been set aside by order of the U.S. Forester, but the order must be confirmed by Congressional action before funds for purchase of the ranch lands can be made available and it will probably be very difficult, at this time, to secure appropriations or donations. I shall assist George S. [William's brother] wherever I can in 'Stony's' interest but the purchase of a back country ranch under conditions existing here, at present, will be very difficult to make. The Forest Service may be able to buy his mules and horses but their value is very low now."[92]

Many of the inholdings within the Idaho Primitive Area and adjacent surrounding National Forest lands in central Idaho were

---

91 There was public fear and vocal opposition to the government allocating funds to purchase private inholdings within the Idaho Primitive Area during its creation. For specific examples of people and places, especially those related to the Big Creek drainage see Dr. G. Wayne Minshall's *Cabin Creek Chronicle: The History of the Most Remote Ranch in America.* Inkom, ID: Streamside Scribe Press, 2014. 125-146.

92 Harry C. Shellworth. Letter to Mr. J.O. Stewart. 28 October 1932. Harry C. Shellworth Collection MS-269, Idaho State Historical Society Archives.

purchased by the Idaho Department of Fish and Game in the 1940s (including the Stonebraker Ranch), most of which they retain at the time of this writing for field research and to facilitate sportsman access. However, it was not until the 1970s, when the Idaho Primitive Area was being managed as a "Wilderness Study Area," that the federal government acknowledged the direction originally outlined in the 1931 Idaho Primitive Area plan to purchase inholdings as they became available for sale. This especially became evident in the Big Creek drainage as six original homesteads were acquired by the Forest Service between 1970 and 1979 with the intent to fully remove all improvements and naturalize the sites.

As for the second issue—regarding the use of airplanes in the Idaho Primitive Area—it can be postulated based on the meager space given to the topic in the 1931 *Idaho Primitive Area Report* that no one foresaw the substantial impact the use of aircraft would ultimately have.[93] It is important to note that very few people had the means or the skills to operate aircraft privately in the 1920s and 1930s, and the few commercial operators who were flying in the primitive areas were only supplementing their income by transporting sportsmen. The commercial operator's bread and butter stemmed from government contracts with the Forest Service in the all-out fight against wildfire during the summer months. These flights were aerial fire patrols, moving men and equipment in and out of remote regions once thought nearly inaccessible except by several days on horseback. It is clear from the language in the *Idaho Primitive Area Report* that the Forest Service was in support of the development of aircraft landing

---

93 The 1931 *Idaho Primitive Area Report* was compiled by compiled by Forest Supervisor S. C. Scribner and approved by Regional Forester R.H. Rutledge and forester R. Y. Stuart.

fields for their own administrative uses: "There exists among sports-men and others a strong feeling that the use of airplanes in hunting should be prohibited. It is felt that these objections are well founded and that the development of landing fields within the area should be prohibited excepting, perhaps, two or three that may be needed for emergency landings or in fire control work."[94] However, one can gather from the report that the general view was that for the public aviator or sportsman, access to the area should be limited, as the report states, "If auto travel is not to be condoned, surely entrance by air should also be discouraged."[95]

In reality, the Forest Service did not discourage public use of its airfields, and as an agency it was sold on airstrips throughout central Idaho to combat wildland fire, especially in the hinterlands of the Idaho Primitive Area. In the region of central Idaho the agency constructed on average at least one backcountry airstrip per year from 1930 to 1941. Within the boundaries of the area designated as the Idaho Primitive Area the agency developed between 1925 to 1941 ten airstrips, and private land owners developed five others. However, post-World War II the inverse occurred, as the Forest Service gradually moved away from the direct use of the airstrips in fire suppression activities and instead expanded smokejumper programs and deployed technology developed during the war such as helicopters and retardants; fire "control" changed to fire "management." On the flip side of this equation, the owners of private inholdings built more airstrips for access—six more between 1945-1964.

---

94   S.C. Scribner. *Idaho Primitive Area Report*. USDA, Forest Service: 17 March 1931. 22. Holm Collection.

95   Scribner, 22.

Within the first decade following Harry's great success with the Idaho Primitive Area designation, the place began to change. Air traffic increased and Harry's primitive area friends, who called the remote mountains home, slowly passed away. Stonebraker died in 1932.[96] Dave Lewis sold his ranch to Jess and Dorothy Taylor in 1934 and died two years later.[97] Profile Sam, who Harry loved to tell the story of supplying with a still, died in October 1934.[98] The Edward's guest operation at the head of Big Creek closed in the mid 1930s. The Elliott brothers, who owned a ranch on Big Creek, were gone by the late 1930s.[99]

---

96 Stonebraker died of a heart attack at age fifty-three in September 1932. He was on his way out from the ranch for supplies and he was breaking camp in the morning, twelve miles from the Werdenhoff Mine. He sat down to enjoy his tobacco pipe, when he experienced heart pain and fell over. His stepson Bill rode to the Chicken Peak Fire Lookout to get word out that he had died. His body was packed back to the ranch and flown by pilots Bob King and Stonebraker's brother George Jr. to Lewiston (where he was buried).

97 Pat Cary Peek's book *Cougar Dave: Mountain Man of Idaho*. Bend, OR: Maverick Publications, 2004, is considered the most complete source on Dave Lewis's life. The book includes several references to Lewis's friendship with Harry Shellworth. Jess Taylor sold the ranch to the University of Idaho in 1969. Since then the property has functioned as a year-round wilderness field station. Today ongoing work continues, involving universities, scientists, professors, and students in the areas of wildlife, stream ecology, fisheries, plant ecology, soils, and anthropology. The University of Idaho Library Special Collections also houses the papers of Dave Lewis (MG 190).

98 Samuel Willson died of a self-inflicted gunshot wound on October 8, 1934. Willson was a miner and legend has it that he and some of his friends were drinking moonshine when they envisioned the face of the mountain was the profile of George Washington. The name was given to the mountain, which also happened to be the location of Willson's cabin. There is a stone monument to Willson near the road through Profile Gap, which indicates the incorrect death date of 1935.

99 Joe Elliott, who homesteaded the property known today as the Mile High Ranch near Garden Creek on the north side of Big Creek, left the country prior to his brother Ernest "Hardrock" Elliott's death in 1934. Ernest died of Rocky Mountain spotted tick fever and was buried on a knoll above the old ranch building complex. His headstone is still visible. The Elliott family then sold the ranch in 1937.

In May 1937 Harry asserted in a letter to a friend that he had made twenty-six trips into the Idaho Primitive Area.[100] According to his correspondence and his family's recollections, his famous pack trips into his "Dreamland" ended abruptly by the late 1930s. While the changing landscape may have figured in the decline, Harry was no longer a young man; in 1937 he celebrated his sixtieth birthday.

Nothing formally carries Shellworth's name in the Frank Church River of No Return Wilderness, although one unique monument which he helped build exists within its boundaries. As in his time, the area will always be known for the natural geologic features of the Middle Fork of the Salmon River and Big Creek region. However, a headstone/monument marking the grave or once gravesite of Private Harry Eagan at Soldier Bar on the lower portion of Big Creek still stands. The monument was erected in 1925 and Shellworth had a hand in its construction and placement. It is likely one of the more remote military, marble headstones in the world. As one can imagine, the monument was frequently referred to by Harry in his correspondence to people interested in a trip into the Idaho Primitive Area, and was a site he often visited. The distinctive high-bench formation of Soldier Bar along the south side of the river was used frequently by the Northern Shoshone. On August 19, 1879, during the Sheepeater Indian conflict, while the US Army was attempting to remove the remaining indigenous inhabitants from the area, a skirmish erupted on the high bar. The Shoshone, who had retreated from their encampment on the bar the previous day, had crept down the rock cliffs from above and attacked. During the altercation Private Harry Eagan was

---

100 Harry C. Shellworth. Letter to Stanly A. Easton. 17 May 1937. Harry C. Shellworth Collection MS-269, Idaho State Historical Society Archives.

shot through both thighs. A doctor came to the aid of the wounded soldier and anesthetized with chloroform in order to amputate his leg. He died during the operation. Eagan was buried at the bar, thus the name Soldier Bar.

When Colonel W.C. Brown retired from the military, he began recording many events that occurred during his career. Included among his writing was the story of the Sheepeater conflict of 1879. Although Eagan was not under his command during the expedition, he thought a memorial should be established at the place to mark the location of the military engagement and the grave. In early 1925 Brown made an inquiry to the Clover postmaster, Joe Elliott who lived at the Mile High Ranch situated on the north side of Big Creek about seven miles from the river's confluence with the Middle Fork about the location of Eagan's grave. It is thought that Elliott, helped to establish a correspondence between Brown and Harry's good friend, Dave Lewis, who worked for a packer hired by the Army during the Sheepeater conflict. Several letters and notes about the project were exchanged among the three men over several months.[101] In one of Lewis's letters to Brown, he verified that he could show him the exact location of the gravesite. However, he expressed some doubt that Eagan's remains were still present, stating, "I always understood that in a year or so, his remains were taken up & sent to Boise, or elsewhere. It was 20 yrs. after the battle at Soldier Bar, before I came back into the Big Creek country...At any rate the grave was opened

101 Harry Eagan Burial File. National Archives, RG92, Stack Area 3/70, Row 65, Compartment 11, Shelf 7, Box 1458.

& shows it to this day."[102] Brown, apparently satisfied with Lewis's knowledge of the grave's location, persuaded the US Army to fund the Soldier Bar monument.[103]

Following the standard protocol set by the United States, an order was placed with the Vermont Marble Company of Proctor, Vermont, to make a headstone for Eagan. The military's World War I design was slightly modified at Brown's request to include extra lettering on the stone to give some explanation of the events surrounding Eagan's death. Due to the stone's proposed isolated location, the War Department's Construction Service designed the special conical base for the headstone.[104]

With arrangements made between Brown and Elliott, the US Army hired Elliott to transport the material for the monument and to build it. On June 15, 1925 the stone was shipped from Vermont to Boston, Massachusetts, where it was placed on a steamship and taken to Portland, Oregon. From Portland it was delivered by rail to McCall on September 4. Elliott then hauled the three-hundred-pound stone by wagon to Edwardsburg via Warren, and then packed it the remainder of the way to Soldier Bar, along with all the necessary construction materials.[105]

On Elliott's way to Soldier Bar he stopped at the Lewis Ranch, where Harry was staying with Dave as part of his annual backcountry trip. The two offered to help build the monument and by the end of

102 David Lewis. Letter to Col. W.C. Brown. 1 February 1925. W.C. Brown Collection, University of Colorado at Boulder Archives.

103 Eagan Burial File.

104 Eagan Burial File.

105 Eagan Burial File.

October, it was completed. Some quibbling between Elliott and the US Army occurred over the costs of transportation and construction, which totaled to $281.10. One Army individual wrote Elliott, "The request to do this work is not made so much on account of any small profit or pay which may be gotten for the work as through patriotic interest." In a response letter, Elliott threw in his own jabs and made comments such as, "It all takes time in a country like this" and "I always try to be as patriotic as the next one." He even recognized Harry in the same letter, writing, "With the kind and able assistance of Mr. Harry Shellworth (one of the head men of Boise Payette Lumber Co.) I was able to put the marble stone in place and cement it there. At any time I will be glad to refer you to Mr. Shellowrth, Boise, Idaho concerning this monument." All matters were eventually dropped and at the urging of Colonel W.C. Brown in January 1926 the military sent Harry a personal letter thanking him for his help, remarking, "Your helpful interest in this matter is much appreciated, and I am instructed to convey to you the thanks of this office, Very truly yours, L.W. Redington."[106]

---

106 Eagan Burial File.

DAVE LEWIS AND HARRY AT LEWIS RANCH LOWER BIG CREEK 1920S.
(Shellworth Family Collection)

HARRY'S IDAHO PRIMITIVE AREA DEPOSIT
SLIP POUCH FOR TOILET PAPER.
*(Harry C. Shellworth Collection MS-269 Idaho State
Historical Society Archives/Holm photograph)*

SHELLWORTH'S 1927 BACKCOUNTRY TRIP, WEST FORK OF RUSH
CREEK, TRIBUTARY TO BIG CREEK NEAR LEWIS RANCH. LEFT
TO RIGHT: UNKNOWN, UNKNOWN, R.H. RUTLEDGE, HARRY,
DAVE LEWIS, "GOLDIE" MOORE, "JEFF" JEFFRIES, ANDY CASNER,
GOVERNOR CLARENCE BALDRIDGE, AND STANLY EASTON.
(Johnson & Son/Idaho State Historical Society MS-269-22)

SOLDIER BAR MONUMENT FRANK CHURCH
RIVER OF NO RETURN. *(Holm photograph)*

HARRY'S REMOTE AND RUGGED "DREAMLAND" FROM 40,000 FEET
LOOKING NORTH-NORTHEAST TOWARD THE MIDDLE FORK SALMON
RIVER. THE BIG CREEK DRAINAGE LOWER LEFT *(Holm photograph)*

Harry penned the following poem in a 1931 thank-you letter to Mr. J.O. Stewart, who had been on one of Shellworth's summer pack trips through the Idaho Primitive Area. In the letter Harry thanks the Stewarts for a photograph they gave him of Stanley Lake that was taken during their Idaho travels, commenting, "It [the photograph] is already in a place of honor among other mountain and lake pictures in our family room. In the picture of Stanley Lake and Stanley Peak you have caught a view I have not heretofore seen and both Mrs. Shellworth and I like it best of any we have seen." He further explains the image inspired him to write a poem (untitled) by noting, "I think the following lines fit it [the photograph] as aptly as anything, except possibly an organ pealed anthem."

Come feast your orbs upon this land,
Of quaking asp, of pine and spruce,
Of thunder storms like hell broke loose,
Of avalanche and snowy slide,
That clear half a mountain side.

The hills that from this rugged vale,
Lift heavenward their slopes of shale,
Their startling crags of contour bold,
Were fashioned in a mighty mold;
No small nor petty thoughts can find,
A welcome in a mortal's mind,
The while there stands before his eyes,
This underpinning of the skies.

6

AUTO TOURS

*Around campfires at night, if the guides have been well chosen,
there will be many a tall tale. There may be a Dave Lewis story
of a cougar, skulking, cowardly and waiting for a deer…Around
campfires, too, there will be much that any man, once he has known
it, will wish to return to, or that any man, never having known it
before, will take to his heart. There will be the smell of pine and
cedar boughs on a friendly fire, fragrance of bacon in a hot skillet,
and of coffee steaming. There will be the smell of old cones and
leaf depths, aspen hillsides, mahogany reaches, and landslides of
stone. Persons who pack into this area know the smell of bear or
rockchuck, of elk beds or beaver slides, goat and golden eagle.*
—VARDIS FISHER
Idaho Guide (1937)

As much as Harry enjoyed his famous pack trips, he also reveled in
taking people on auto tours throughout Idaho's forests. Often these

show-me tours revolved around the entertainment of different forestry groups, boards, and associations to which Harry belonged. The trips were generally highlighted by stops at fire lookouts, scenic overlooks, evening dinner parties at lodges, and included activities such as fishing. Similar to the pack trips, these auto tours were planned by him and often catered to people of influence in political office or industry. Of the dozens of trips, two in particular illustrate this aspect of Harry's life.

The earlier of these two trips occurred in the summer of 1927 at the time Senator Borah was contemplating running as a Republican candidate in the 1928 presidential race. As mentioned, Borah and Harry met through John Blake, and forged a personal friendship and business relationship that lasted throughout their lives. Borah has remained one of the most recognized Idaho politicians—earning national notoriety in mid-1907 as the prosecutor in the trial of Big Bill Haywood. Haywood was tried for conspiracy in the murder of ex-Idaho Governor Frank Steunenberg. Even though Haywood was acquitted, the trial transformed Borah from an unrecognized Senator to a national figure. He served as a US Senator from 1907 until his death in January 1940.

The Borah-Shellworth auto tour trip was funded by Borah's closest friend and confidant C.C. Anderson, who owned a department store in downtown Boise. The trip was made in three automobiles from Boise with the destination of the small mining outpost at the headwaters of Big Creek. The group was comprised of Anderson and his wife and two nephews, Borah and his wife, Harry and his son Eugene, Arthur Coonrod (SITPA chief fire warden), and photographer Ansgar Johnson. The tour went by way of Smiths Ferry, McCall, Warren, South Fork of the Salmon River, over Elk Creek Summit, and down to Big Creek. They stayed several days with the William

Edwards family, who ran a guest lodge and store in the remote community named Edwardsburg after the family.[107] The purpose of the tour was to gather some publicity photographs showing Borah fishing, riding horses, and being in the outdoors.

The idea was to take photographs of Borah that would portray him as another Teddy Roosevelt, or as Harry phrased it, "his hero picture." Each evening the group gathered to discuss the day's events and most importantly mull over Borah's decision to run for president. Borah often introduced Harry among political peers as "Idaho's politician anonymous." Summing up their relationship Harry noted, "I knew if Borah wanted any information from me he'd ask for it, and I knew if I wanted anything from him I could ask for it." Regarding the last evening of the trip Harry recalled, "On Edwards' house porch, the last evening, during our final talk Borah asked me what I thought was his worst handicap. Remembering Funston's failure to make the grade, I answered, 'Political Geography'...Borah turned to Anderson and said, 'C.C. that's it.' A very short time after that Borah announced that he was not a candidate." There was more to the decision, because Borah himself doubted he could win enough delegates at the Republican Convention. Borah biographer Marian C. McKenna recognizes this moment as one of the most pivotal in Borah's career, "As events ran their course, Borah aspired to become not president but a western Warwick; he hoped not only to name the Republican candidate for president but dictate the platform of 1928 as well, and thus become a power behind the throne."[108]

---

107 At the time of this writing the Edwards' home where the Borah-Shellworth party stayed is standing in ruins on private property at its original location on the south side of Logan Creek in Edwardsburg proper. The most visible portion of the ruins is the front porch.

108 McKenna, 251-53.

Although the trip resulted in Borah opting out of the 1928 presidential campaign, the auto tour produced a stunning collection of candid photographs of everyone on the trip, many of which appeared in national newspapers. In gratitude, Anderson hired Ansgar Johnson, Sr., to produce three large photo albums of the trip with colored tinting on each of them complete with detailed captions. One of the books was kept by Anderson, the others kept by Borah and Harry.[109]

The second noteworthy Shellworth guided auto tour transpired thirteen years after the Borah trip, and was into another of Harry's favorite areas—the Stanley Basin. In June 1936, R.E. Shepherd, the president of the Idaho Chamber of Commerce, contacted Harry (chamber board member) and Richard Rutledge, a regional forester with the Intermountain Region of the US Forest Service, at the suggestion of Borah, to see if they could put together a late summer show-me trip in the mountains north of Ketchum for Union Pacific Railroad President Carl Gray and other railroad directors and board members. Gray and many of the executives were interested in seeing the site of the UP Railroad's new destination resort, Sun Valley, which had just broken ground. The purpose of the new resort was to provide a journey's end, thus increasing ridership on UP rail lines in the western United States. Rutledge was very influential at the federal level, and had worked closely with Harry on the establishment of the Idaho Primitive Area, and maintained a close friendship. Harry enthusiastically responded to Shepherd's request, "I shall be glad indeed to help in any way I can as, like you, I feel that this is an opportunity we

---

109 Harry donated his photo album of the trip to the Idaho State Historical Society in 1966, where it remains in their archives (Harry Shellworth Album) Borah G35 (63-219).

must not overlook… Also, when you know the names of those in the party, give me a list and I will arrange Primitive Area Deposit Slip packets for them, which will help to start off the party with a joke. I certainly hope Dick Rutledge will be able to go also, as he will be a material factor in the success of the trip in assuring us of the active assistance en route of all forest officials, I believe we can arrange an automobile trip that will astound Mr. Gray and his party."[110] Rutledge had originally planned on attending, but his schedule was busy and in the end he was unable to make the trip.

However, in correspondence with Shepherd he wrote, "I know also that Harry Shellworth will be of great assistance in planning the trip and carrying it out. I certainly appreciate the invitation you have given me."[111] Rutledge also connected Shellworth and Shepherd with several other US Forest Service officials to contribute to the trip, including F.S. Moore, supervisor of the Sawtooth National Forest, C.N. Woods, assistant regional forester, and E.E. McKee, supervisor of the Challis National Forest.

With the itinerary set for July 10, the first part of the group met at the Pocatello UP train station. Harry drove his car from Boise and met them, along with other Idaho representatives; at the UP train station in Shoshone. The group and its luggage were divided up among the automobiles and they set off for Ketchum. When venturing out into the woods, especially for work, Harry drove a utilitarian, trusty pickup, but for auto tours and long drives

---

110 Harry C. Shellworth. Letter to Mr. R.E. Shepherd. 27 June 1936. Harry C. Shellworth Collection MS-269, Idaho State Historical Society Archives.

111 R.H. Rutledge. Letter to Mr. R. E. Shepherd. 26 June 1936. Harry C. Shellworth Collection MS-269, Idaho State Historical Society Archives.

he drove his personal car—a comfortable automobile for Harry meant a convertible, and typically a Buick. For this trip he drove a relatively new Buick convertible coupe. Admiring the sleek lines of the convertible at the train station, Gray opted to ride with Harry for the first leg to Ketchum. Both with a gift of gab, the two men hit it off. It was not long into the drive when they figured out their paths had crossed forty years earlier on the *S. S. Santa Ana*, when Harry was a cabin boy and Gray a passenger. Gray was traveling under an assumed name to survey the Santa Ana Line and territory as part of a prospective purchase for the railroad. Their chance encounter decades earlier was confirmed when both collaborated on telling the same story of being in Hell's Kitchen, a combination theater and saloon in Panama City, on the night a local bandit, "Pablo San Antonio" and his men, vamoosed with a group of female dancers from the stage and high-tailed it to their mountain hideaway.[112] Mutually recounting the story made the two men fast friends. Through this connection, Gray gained a level of trust and comradery.

Journeying northward along the rising foothills south of Hailey, Shellworth and Gray continually talked. It became apparent to Harry that the UP stockholders were very concerned about the Sun Valley investment; after all, in their minds it was in the middle of nowhere: Idaho. Some of the stockholders even believed that "Averell Harriman had 'sold his father something' in this ski resort deal."[113] The purpose of Gray's trip was to investigate the construction and the general

---

112 Harry C. Shellworth interview by Elwood R. Maunder, Version #2, 22-23.

113 Harry C. Shellworth, interview by Elwood R. Maunder, Version #2, 22.

area of Sun Valley in order to gain an understanding of the project and offer reassurance to the stockholders and company. At the time of the trip, the concrete was just beginning to be poured for the first floor of the two-hundred-plus room hotel. When finished, the cost of the resort was estimated to be $750,000.[114]

With not much to see at the site of the lodge and the resort grounds, except some concrete footings and wooden stakes, the group set off to find guest accommodations in Hailey, but none could be found. Apparently, a mix-up had occurred among the UP officials regarding who was to book the reservations. One of the men from the Salt Lake City office then decided to be the hero and telephoned the Idaho Rocky Mountain Club seventy-five miles north in the Stanley Basin. The owner of the dude ranch operation, Paul Winston, answered and after a brief discussion explained that they were not a commercial resort designed to accommodate such a party. Desperate, the UP man explained the situation to Harry, who just smiled, he knew Winston well. The Idaho Rocky Mountain Club was a regular stopover for Harry when he was in the Stanley area traveling or fishing, and he greatly admired the outdoor skills of the manager and the lead guide there, Claude Gillespie. Winston, a New York Frigidaire distributor, purchased the ranch for hunting in 1929.[115] It just so happened that Harry had recently helped Winston acquire two-hundred acres of state land in the vicinity of the lodge's main water supply. Winston

---

114 "Gray Inspects Stanley Basin: President of Union Pacific party Interested in Resort Development," *The Idaho Daily Statesman*, 11 July 1936. For more information on the history of Sun Valley see: Wendolyn Holland, *Sun Valley: An Extraordinary History*, (Nampa, ID: The Idaho Press, 1998).

115 The Idaho Rocky Mountain Club was listed on the National Register of Historic Places in 1994. For a complete history of the property see: Linda Morton-Keithley, National Register of Historic Places Registration Form —#94001451, 9 December 1994.

obviously owed Harry a favor and Harry collected. Again, the call was brief, but the outcome was different. And so, with Harry's connections, the Idaho Rocky Mountain Club became the base of operations for the rest of the UP party's multi-day Idaho trip. The group was extremely taken by the beauty of the Stanley Basin and the grandeur of the Sawtooth Mountain Range.[116]

As guests at the Club, the group ventured about by automobiles to the Sawtooth lakes accessible by road, and walked the shores of Alturas, Pettit, and Redfish lakes.[117] Day trips were made along the Salmon River, and Harry even squeezed in a trip to visit Feltham Creek Point fire lookout on the divide between the Middle Fork of Salmon River country and Stanley Basin for exceptional views into his Idaho Primitive Area.[118] Reflecting about the trip in 1963, Harry recalled the group standing on the summit near the fire lookout with a 360-degree panorama of some of the most magnificent mountains in the United States, from the lesser known Tangos to the Boulder White Clouds to the Sawtooths. Harry sensed this was the lynchpin moment when Gray and the other UP executives felt confident about the Sun Valley business decision. Harry concluded, "It seemed to reassure them in regard to the whole Sun Valley project. The day was clear. I told them that from this lookout you could see Montana and Oregon and Washington with field glasses. And Gray walked

---

116 Harry C. Shellworth, interview by Ralph W. Hidy, 81-82.

117 *Memoirs July 1936 H. Shellworth: Union Pacific Railroad, Sun Valley, Carl Gray Party.* This is a several page photograph album of the trip with labeled images. Harry C. Shellworth Collection MS-269, Idaho State Historical Society Archives.

118 Feltham Creek Point was a US Forest Service lookout constructed in 1933 and removed in 1967. The road to the lookout site still exists and concrete footings of the former building are evident.

over to Schmidt, Gray's assistant, and said, 'Do you hear that, it's Tremendous!!!'"[119]

Carl Gray retired before the grand opening of the resort, but as a thank-you to Harry, he passed on to his successor, William Jeffers, a "must invitation list," including Mr. and Mrs. Harry Shellworth. The finished resort exceeded any before—with circle-shaped swimming pools, the world's first automated chairlift, and multiple lodges. As part of the grand opening, the railroad hosted a multi-day convention and Harry was there. The gala was mainly attended by UP Railroad stockholders from New York. However, for the last two days Stella joined Harry, along with other local invitees Joel L. Priest, a UP Railroad Boise employee, and Charlie Davidson, a friend of the Shellworths who had driven Stella to Sun Valley.[120] Davidson, a Harvard-trained landscape architect, designed the grounds around the Sun Valley Lodge, in a style similar to his personal gardens developed in McCall on Sylvan Creek. He also designed the Trail Creek Lodge for the Resort.[121] At the main celebration dinner, the Shellworths sat at Jeffers' table with Idaho Governor Ben Ross. As for Harry's personal thoughts on his small part in promoting the state's most recognizable international resort in the summer of 1936, he commented, "I do know that Gray was very much pleased and that, as far as I could judge the comments of the other members, their reports should have been complete approval. I do know that Mr. Shepherd, President of the Idaho State Chamber of Commerce and Mr. C.A.

---

119 Harry C. Shellworth, interview by Elwood R. Maunder, Version #2, 23.

120 Harry C. Shellworth, interview by Ralph W. Hidy, 83.

121 Margaret Gorrissen. Personal Communication. 8 May 2020. Margaret is the granddaughter of Charlie Davidson.

Barton, Manager of the Boise Payette Lumber Co., both received letters complimenting my M.C. abilities and knowledge of Idaho's mountains etc. I have always been highly allergic to 'Corral Dust' but this time, it wasn't hard to take."[122]

WILLIAM BORAH, CENTER, HARRY, RIGHT, ELK CREEK SUMMIT EN ROUTE TO HEADWATERS OF BIG CREEK AND EDWARDSBURG 1927. *(Johnson & Son/Idaho State Historical Society Shellworth Photo Album #6-11)*

---

122 Harry C. Shellworth, interview by Ralph W. Hidy, 84.

THE UNION PACIFIC AUTO-TOUR GROUP JUNE 1936, SUMMIT OF
FELTHAM CREEK POINT, TANGO MOUNTAINS BACKGROUND.
BACK ROW LEFT TO RIGHT: C.N. WOODS (ASSOCIATE REGIONAL
FORESTER), R.E. SHEPHERD (PRESIDENT OF THE IDAHO STATE
CHAMBER OF COMMERCE), CARL GRAY (PRESIDENT OF THE
UNION PACIFIC RAILROAD), PAUL WINSTON (OWNER OF THE
IDAHO ROCKY MOUNTAIN CLUB), J.E. HAUGH (ASSISTANT
TO GRAY), J.A. SEITZ (UNION PACIFIC SALT LAKE OFFICE),
E.C. SCHMIDT (ASSISTANT TO GRAY), AND F.S. MOORE
(SUPERVISOR OF THE SAWTOOTH NATIONAL FOREST).
FRONT ROW LEFT TO RIGHT: CLARK HEISE, R.P. PARRY, E.E.
MCKEE (ACTING SUPERVISOR OF THE CHALLIS NATIONAL
FOREST), F.J. MELIA (ASSISTANT TO GRAY), HARRY, AND CLAUDE
GILLESPIE (MANAGER OF THE IDAHO ROCKY MOUNTAIN CLUB).
(Shellworth Family Collection)

7

IDAHO'S TRAVEL AUTHORITARIAN AND HISTORIAN ANONYMOUS

The enormous landscape eastward is not only a wilderness [the Idaho Primitive Area] of peaks and canyons and streams. It is also a wilderness of legend, of doings both fabulous and real, with the truth of them deferring to drama and getting lost in the telling.
—VARDIS FISHER
Idaho Guide (1937)

Harry contributed to Idaho culturally, by preserving the history of the West Central Mountains and the Idaho Primitive Area. At a young age, history and geography were the only subjects that Harry cared for, interests that stuck with him for the rest of his life. In retrospect he admitted that he did not take to reading and literature until later in life. As he matured his preferences ranged from travel stories to history, and studying "great speeches."

Explaining his thoughts on what reading and books meant to him he said, "You could see the world. You might say that was the leading urge."[123] Whenever the opportunity arose for him to contribute to the literature written about the places he cherished in Idaho, he gladly did so. Harry profoundly understood the delicate balance of generating public interest in the Idaho Primitive Area, without promoting overuse or commercialization. In an era when public land was valued for its productivity (timber, mining, grazing, leisure), the public had to have a personal stake, even if the connection was just reading about it.

Over the course of Harry's roughly thirty-some pack trips, he picked up a lot of first and second-hand historical knowledge of the area. In essence, if you wanted to know anything about the Idaho Primitive Area, from planning a sightseeing trip, fishing trip, hunting trip, or merely learn a story, Harry was the man. Through his role as the expert on the area, he fostered several relationships with well-known authors and journalists who preserved some of the area's oral history. Northwest writer Stewart Holbrook, who described himself as a "low-brow" historian with an interest in what he coined the "Far Corner" (Washington, Oregon, and Idaho), corresponded with Harry about Idaho history. Holbrook published more than thirty books and regularly wrote for *The Oregonian*, the Portland daily newspaper. Two of his books contain Idaho-related material passed on by Harry:

---

123 Harry C. Shellworth, interview by Elwood R. Maunder, Version #1, 13.

Burning an Empire (1943) and *Rocky Mountain Revolution* (1956).[124]

Another author hooked by Harry and his backcountry stories was Anne O'Hare McCormick, a journalist with *The New York Times*. The two met when she came to Idaho to interview US Senator Borah. During the same trip, Harry escorted her and her husband/manager Francis on a scenic tour of the Boise Front, with a stop at the Shafer Butte Fire Lookout. As a result of that encounter, Harry assisted her in writing an extensive piece about the big Idaho forest fires of 1931 titled, "An American Epic in Sand and Flame." The article first appeared as a full-length spread in the October 18, 1931, edition of *The New York Times Magazine*, with photographs by Johnson & Son. Harry later published the story and pictures through SITPA as a fourteen-page booklet. After the success of the "Epic" article, McCormick and Harry exchanged letters in 1932 and 1933 regarding a full-length piece and possibly a book about the history of the Idaho Primitive Area. She had an ardent interest in the history of the area, especially the Thunder Mountain Gold Rush, and the subsequent landslide that destroyed the community of Roosevelt in May 1909. Nothing came of the collaboration and in March 1933 Francis wrote Harry on his wife's behalf, commenting, "She appreciates the compliment you have paid to her and is impressed by the immense and

---

124 Much of the Holbrook correspondence in Shellworth's personal papers regards the Steunenberg trial of which Harry likely relayed the information given to him from his wife and in-laws. Some of the Steunenberg-related material was used in *Rocky Mountain Revolution*. Holbrook also took a great interest in Harry's stories about Jeanette Burgdorf an eccentric woman who resided at the homestead known today as Burgdorf Hot Springs, located thirty miles north of McCall. The hot springs was a popular stopping place on Harry's auto tours. Along with being a genuine backcountry character, Jeanette was a former opera singer. In 1942 Holbrook toyed with the idea of writing a full length chapter on Jeanette's life; however, it did not materialize. He also considered writing of her experiences in connection with the 1919 wildland fires in *Burning an Empire*, which also did not materialize.

orderly knowledge you have of the Primitive Area and your vision of what it can mean to the nation where all areas are so rapidly being checkerboarded by contemporaneous life. Of course, until the country begins to work out of this present crisis not much can be done to further this objective. Mrs. McCormick, herself, is considering an assignment which may take her, accompanied by me, to Europe by the end of this month. These are days, indeed, when one can long for the security and rewards of a primitive area and where one doesn't need to worry about bank holidays and industrial break-down, and so we Easterners covet the release and relief that is at your doorstep."[125] Based on the existing materials from Harry's personal files it appears this ends his correspondence with the McCormicks.[126]

A few years later Harry was contacted by author Vardis Fisher and a friendship quickly grew between them.[127] Through this connection Harry made significant cultural contributions to preserving the history and lore of the Idaho Primitive Area and other surrounding wildlands. Fisher had recently been hired by the Federal Writers' Project (FWP), a sub-program of the Works Progress Administration's (WPA) larger Federal Arts Project aimed at providing economic stimulus for unemployed writers, beginning in 1935. The program specifically

---

125 Francis J. McCormick. Letter to Mr. Harry C. Shellworth. 6 March 1933. Shellworth Family Collection.

126 Anne O'Hara McCormick did in fact take the assignment in Europe mentioned in her husband's letter and her career skyrocketed. From 1933 to 1940, McCormick secured interviews with major world leaders such as Benito Mussolini, Adolf Hitler, Joseph Stalin, Winston Churchill, and Franklin Roosevelt. In 1937 she was awarded the Pulitzer Prize for her work in Europe.

127 The most complete source for information on Vardis Fisher is Tim Woodward's book, *Tiger on the Road: The Life of Vardis Fisher.* Caldwell, ID: Caxton Printers, 1989. For a literary review of Fisher's work see Wayne Chatterton's *Vardis Fisher: The Frontier and Regional Works.* Western Writers Series—Boise State College, 1972.

funded visual arts in the United States. For writers, one of the main goals was to create guidebooks for each state. Initially, Fisher was reluctant to take the government job, but he was nearly broke and felt he had no better options. With six published novels and experience teaching English at the University of Utah, he was an accomplished writer. When he began he had no staff and was told by directors in Washington, D.C., to hire other Idaho writers in need of a job. Trying to explain there were no "writers" to employ was fruitless. Eventually, he was assigned a small staff, one not large enough to produce the desired products: a large guidebook covering the entire state of Idaho for the American Guide Series.

In the nine years the FWP operated, it produced more than four-hundred publications. The volumes covered every state in the union, as well as specific regions, villages, towns, and cities. Under the federal guidelines the contributing authors were to remain anonymous because the books represented a collective effort. Unlike most of the other Guide Series' books, the Idaho edition was written almost entirely by Fisher himself (374 of the 405 pages). And much to the irritation of his superiors, he completed it in an astonishing fourteen months. *Idaho: a Guide in Word and Picture* was the first of the Guide Series books to be published and in many ways became the template for the state books.[128] True to its title, it is a guide that features selected auto tours throughout the state, but it is also literary, and contains a selection of essays on diverse topics. Blended into the

---

128 First edition copies (January 1937) of the *Idaho Guide* are rare because most of the first printing was destroyed by fire in a Caxton warehouse. The second printing (June 1937) followed quickly and is distinguishable by the addition of Vardis Fisher's name on the title page and the inclusion of a folding map at the rear. The book was reprinted in a smaller format by Oxford University Press in 1950. Significant to the Oxford printing is the inclusion of an index.

tours and essays are history and economic promotion of the state's industry and tourism opportunities.[129]

How did Vardis Fisher accomplish the next to impossible? One of the keys was gaining the support of people in the state, who volunteered to do research and donated materials such as news clippings and photographs. As a supporter and advocate for Idaho, Harry actively shared his knowledge, particularly about the Idaho Primitive Area. Fisher was clearly impressed with him, as the Idaho Primitive Area is the subject of two of the fourteen essays—"The Primitive Area" and "A Trip into the Area." Other than the writing, the information is obviously from Harry. The locations are his favorite haunts, and the essays mention a number of his backcountry friends. The book is even peppered with several of Harry's personal photographs, counting one unlabeled cameo appearance among a group of hunters. His influence resulted in more coverage of the Idaho Primitive Area than any other region or topic in the state.

With a turbulent relationship with the main office in Washington, D.C., Fisher left his government position in November 1938 to focus on his personal writing.[130] He went on to publish more than thirty-five books, but before leaving his position he produced two other volumes

---

129 The most definitive source on specifically the *Idaho Guide* is Ronald W. Taber's article, "Vardis Fisher and the 'Idaho Guide,'" *Pacific Northwest Quarterly*. April 1968. 68-76.

130 For more information on FWP see *WPA Guides: Mapping America*, (Jackson, MS: University Press of Mississippi, 1999) by Christine Bold. This source contains details and documentation of the FWP, including a chapter dedicated to Fisher and his efforts in Idaho. However, Bold is overly critical of the *Idaho Guide*. Interestingly, much of her negative critique focuses on the two chapters revolving around the Idaho Primitive Area, and therefore are indirectly a criticism of Harry Shellworth. One of the many unfounded criticisms by Bold includes her analysis of Fisher's oversight on gender diversity by pointing to a picture from one of Harry's pack trips of the naturally formed monument on Monumental Creek, stating, "It is no accident that the most explicitly phallic symbol of the book appears in this section."

for the FWP: *The Idaho Encyclopedia* (1938) and *Idaho Lore* (1939). Both volumes acknowledge Harry Shellworth as one of the many contributors.[131] However, the latter works did not compare in quality and longevity to *Idaho: A Guide in Word and Picture*. Concerning the iconic Idaho book, western writer Ivan Doig said, "[N]either [*The Idaho Encyclopedia* nor *Idaho Lore*] took on a life of its own as the *Idaho Guide* did. Nor, really, did anything else he wrote from then until his death in 1968...Perhaps nothing could have equaled what he managed with *Idaho Guide*. Somehow Fisher's prose, so often overwrought, had been simmered to lively narrative. All his skeptical erudition animated Idaho's history."[132]

Though the *Idaho Guide* clearly stands out as the best example of Harry's cultural contribution to Idaho; he was mentioned in or provided information for countless newspaper articles nationwide, and dozens of national magazines. One extensive article on the state of Idaho by D. Worth Clark in the June 1944 issue of the *National Geographic* touches on all of Harry's favorite subjects: logging, conservation, preservation, wildland fire, primitive areas, politics, Payette Lake and history.[133] The article pins Harry as "[A] real Idaho timber-

---

131 One additional lost manuscript written by Fisher during his time with the FWP was discovered in 2018 at the National Archives in Washington, D.C., by Boise State University archivist Alessandro Meregaglia. The unpublished work, simply titled *Boise Guide*, was posthumously published in 2020 by Rediscovered Publishing of Boise.

132 Ivan Doig. "The Baedeker of Idaho." *Pacific Search: Northwest Nature and Life*. June 1978, 21-23.

133 D. Worth Clark was a political friend of Harry's from Idaho who served two terms as a Democratic US Congressman (1934 and 1936) and two terms as a US Senator (1938 and 1950). Clark's family was well-known in Idaho politics and included two uncles who served as governors (Barzilla Clark and Chase Clark). His cousin, Bethine (Chase Clark's daughter) was married to US Senator Frank Church. The *National Geographic* article was likely part of his 1944 campaign while running for reelection, which he lost to Glen Taylor. Clark was also a member of the National Geographic's expedition down the main Salmon River in 1935.

man, a mighty deer hunter, a booster for the Primitive Areas, and a leader in the campaign against wasteful logging. Knowing virtually all the old-timers in the State, he can spin by the hour 'tall tales' of early days …"[134]

Several years before the *National Geographic* article, Harry was contacted by Metro Goldwyn Mayer studios of Hollywood, California. The studio was working on the adaptation of Kenneth Roberts' *Northwest Passage* novel into a movie, and was scouting possible shooting locations. They solicited Harry's help to determine if suitable locales could be found in Idaho in the areas he was familiar with.

In April 1938 a crew of ten men from the studio arrived in Boise, and was met by Harry along with other knowledgeable Idahoans such as Senator Carl Brown, L.F. Parsons with the Idaho State Chamber of Commerce, and Idaho State Forester Franklin Girard. Harry was enlisted to show them around the Payette Lakes region; the men were lodged at cabins on the west side of Payette Lake at Sylvan Beach. While in McCall, *The Idaho Daily Statesman* reported that arrangements were being made to fly some of the studio personnel in McCall on an aerial tour, which would include the Idaho Primitive Area. Before and after visiting McCall, the Hollywood crew tested shots near Sun Valley, Stanley, Lake Pend 'Oreille, and in the neighboring state of Washington at Lake Chelan and the Columbia River. In the early stages, the planned film cast starred Wallace Beery, Robert Taylor, Clarke Gable, Spencer Tracy, and Gary Cooper. Most notable in the early cast, concerning Harry and Idaho, was Wallace Beery. According to the same newspaper article, "Selection of some place

134 D. Worth Clark. "Idaho Made the Desert Bloom." *The National Geographic Magazine.* June 1944, 665.

in Idaho as the scene for Kenneth Roberts' popular historical novel has the moral support of the state's adopted citizen, Wallace Beery. While he is only a member of the cast and has no say on where the film will be taken, Beery was instrumental in getting the M-G-M scouting party to look over Idaho's possibilities."[135] Not mentioned in the article is Beery's Idaho ownership of a remote historic homestead, known as the Root Ranch, located within the confines of the Idaho Primitive Area. He purchased the remote Chamberlain Basin inholding in 1937 as a hunting getaway.[136] The overwhelmingly similar interests between Beery and Shellworth seem more than coincidental, although no primary documents support the connection.

Interestingly, Beery was struck from the film before shooting began in 1939. However, Harry's sell of the Payette Lakes region must have had some impact, since the film was shot at several locations in the McCall vicinity in 1939-40. Some of the locations were even on land owned by the Boise Payette Lumber Company. Harry interacted with the film crews, as well as the Hollywood stars. He, along with the Carl Brown family, hosted the film director, King Vidor, and several of the stars at the SITPA Statehouse for dinner, and gave tours of the local area, highlighted by stops at SITPA fire lookouts.

---

135 "Movie Scouts Coming Today: Picture Officials to Study McCall Area as Film Site," *The Idaho Daily Statesman*, 26 April 1938.

136 For more information on Beery's Root Ranch property and his time in Idaho see: Richard H. Holm, Jr., *Bound for the Backcountry: A History of Idaho's Remote Airstrips*. McCall, ID: Cold Mountain Press, 2013. 266-68.

DINER HOSTED BY HARRY AND THE BROWNS AT THE
SITPA STATEHOUSE FOR ACTORS AND CREW OF
NORTHWEST PASSAGE 1939. HARRY STANDING,
CARL BROWN SITTING AT FAR END OF TABLE.
CARL'S SON WARREN FRONT RIGHT.
(Johnson & Son/SITPA Collection)

THE CCC-BUILT PACKER JOHN LOOKOUT 1930S.
(Johnson & Son/SITPA Collection)

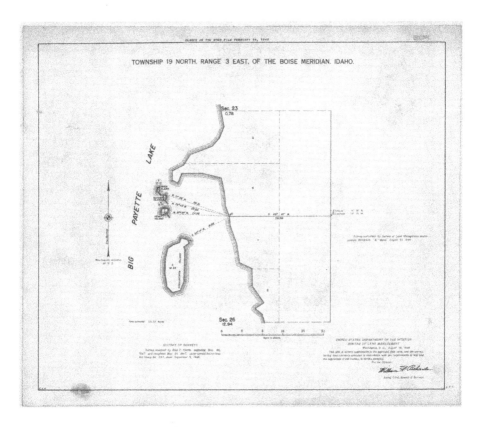

1948 PLAT OF SHELLWORTH ISLAND AND OTHERS
EXTENDING FROM PARADISE POINT. SMALLER ISLANDS
NAMED IN HONOR OF IDAHO EPISCOPALIANS AND THE
BOISE PAYETTE LUMBER COMPANY. SEE FOOTNOTE 145.
(Government Land Office Records)

8
___

LIFE AT BOISE PAYETTE LUMBER COMPANY AND RETIREMENT

*McCall is upon lower Payette Lake in the heart of one of
the State's chief recreation areas. The town itself is rather
unprepossessing, but the lake is as blue as water can be, with shades
varying from delicate pallor to depth that is almost purple.*
—VARDIS FISHER
Idaho Guide (1937)

The 1930s were a time of great personal satisfaction to Harry. He was in the prime of his career—achieving enormous success with his efforts at SITPA and the CCC, and in the midst of it all still finding time for an occasional forest auto tour, fishing or pack trip to the Idaho Primitive Area. However, life at the Boise Payette Lumber Company was anything but rosy. This was a situation Harry rarely publicized but had strong underlying opinions about. The company found some success once the transportation and mill infrastructures were in place, allowing it to be profitable in the years before and after World War I, but the Great Depression hit the company far harder than the other Weyerhaeuser Idaho interests. It was a slump it could never fully recover from during Harry's years with the company. It hit financial rock bottom between 1930 and 1932, reporting average losses at $600,000 annually. Shellworth's superiors fought hard, although they were defeated. C.A. Barton became discouraged, and in failing health resigned in 1931. Sadly, Barton had actually replaced William Carson, who had become similarly crestfallen, just after one year and died.[137]

Lack of key leadership was only one of many problems. Another was the timber market. Boise Payette Lumber Company's inland location could not competitively compete with coastal timber companies that cut year-round and could ship lumber to the East Coast via sea at far cheaper rates. Also there was little market demand for ponderosa or white fir, the primary species of the company's timber stands. Boise Payette, moreover, had the good fortune of buying its timberland at bargain rates, but in the broader picture the actual stands were limited and the land was mostly hemmed in by state-and federally-owned forests, leading to a plethora of other problems. Just when things could not get any worse, bank failures were nearly a final blow because Boise Payette had considerable funds on deposit with First National Bank of Boise, when it closed. Taking on the "sinking ship" was Sumner G. "Jack" Moon and Dr. E.P. Clapp. Moon was

---

137 Hidy et al, 534-35.

well-liked personally and for his business sense. In fact, Harry commented often that Jack was the best person he ever worked for at the company. In an all-out effort to save Boise Payette the administration agreed to economize as much as possible and they all took pay cuts. Some of the retail outlets of the business were closed indefinitely, and several of the mills were temporarily closed, and the Barber Mill near Boise was closed permanently.[138]

In an effort to recover, Moon and Clapp had the company's holdings re-inventoried to determine how much timber could be harvested with selective logging. A retail and public relations campaign was also launched to persuade Midwestern buyers that the yellow color of "yellow pine" was the only drawback to the wood, and it actuality had the same characteristics of the more desirable Douglas fir. To boost desirability of the species, the company referred to it only as "ponderosa." Boise Payette also outsourced logging activities to contractors (J.I. Morgan and MacGregor Logging Company), finding they could do the same job at lower rates. Then, to reduce the freight costs, portable mills were established close to the logging operations, where logs were rough cut and then transported for finishing to the Emmett operation. Just as last-ditch efforts to save the company were starting to pay off, the United States entered World War II and the demand for lumber skyrocketed, which benefited timber companies with supply, but supply was something Boise Payette lacked. When the War Production Board urged all timber companies to increase output; however, Boise Payette could not say "no," as doing so was unpatriotic. Throughout the war years the company kept employment

---

138 Hidy et al, 535-37.

high and earnings higher than they had been for years. The only problem was that it was exhausting the resources and tapping into the timber reserves—ignoring the strong conservation ethics it had prided itself on for years.[139]

Boise Payette emerged into the high-demand post-World War II market with very little marketable resources and an overwhelmed leadership. Since the onset of the Great Depression, Harry and his fellow executives, particularly Jack Moon, had fought the good fight, but obstacle after obstacle and problem after problem had taken its toll. Company morale was very poor. The stamina and determination that once defined Harry and the other executives was gone. Repeatedly, Weyerhaeuser headquarters directed liquidation of the assets. Capturing the mood at that time, historian Ralph W. Hidy quoted a leading man with the company who preferred to remain anonymous, "His [Harry Shellworth's] instructions were to get rid of this land as fast as he could, and he did. Some good bargains were put on the block. We begged people to buy. It was cutover land, but it sure had a lot of virgin timber left up in the corners. The loggers did what they pleased. They were just getting their operation over with. They were trying to clear it up and forget about it."[140] For Harry witnessing the decline of the company he took such pride in was disheartening. Tired and having just celebrated his seventieth birthday, Harry decided in 1947, after more than forty years with the company, to retire.

---

139 Hidy et al, 537-39.

140 Hidy et al, 537-39. Note that the term "cutover" in this era of timber management and logging is misleading because it referred not to a clear cut, but the lack of merchantable timber. For example in the case of Boise Payette Lumber Company the land might be considered "cutover" if all the merchantable ponderosa and white fir had been removed. However, this did not mean that there were not quality stands of other tree species with large diameter specimens—such as spruce, lodgepole, subalpine fir, etc.

In 1949, with the company on the verge of bankruptcy, a surprising turning point occurred. An entirely new group of men came into leadership, most notably John Aram as president, of whom Harry strongly approved. Aram was an Idaho native, having grown up on the Salmon River, graduated from the University of Idaho, and worked his way up in Weyerhaeuser's Potlatch Forests, Inc. in northern Idaho.[141] Aram set forth and executed a new agenda to save the company. First, the company developed sustainable tree farms. Second, the company leased the cutover land to various grazing outfits to generate revenue while new growth matured into harvestable timber. Third, the company began building relationships with the US Forest Service and the state of Idaho for timber sales to feed their mills until the tree farms and existing timber holdings matured. Building the relationships with the latter agencies was challenging, in part because Boise Payette had tarnished its reputation during World War II with unsustainable logging practices. In respect to rapport with the US Forest Service and the state, Harry was given the credit for laying the groundwork. Historian Hidy recognized this writing, "Aram steadily improved Boise Payette relations with the State Land Board and State Forester. The years of hard labor that Harry Shellworth had given to the Western Forestry and Conservation Association assisted Aram in this."[142] Aram continued on with Boise Payette Lumber Company until 1956, when he moved on to a position with Weyerhaeuser Timber Company. Aram's successor, Robert "Bob" Hansberger, led the company through a pivotal merger within

---

141   For more on the Aram family see: Kristi M. Youngdahl. *The Arams of Idaho: Pioneers of Camas Prairie and Joseph Plains.* Moscow, ID: University of Idaho Press, 1995.

142   Hidy et al, 547.

the following year, which created the powerful and successful Boise Cascade Corporation.[143]

Following the Great Depression and turmoil at Boise Payette Lumber Company, the ever persistent and underlying task of asset liquation weighed heavily on Harry as the company's land agent. As a consequence of his job, he in many ways shaped the future development of certain areas in Idaho. And, although the company was in need of money, Harry and Jack Moon recognized a societal obligation to conserve key pieces of land in the interest of spurring local tourism and in some part public access. Harry's tremendous influence in this area is most obvious in the vicinity of the Payette Lakes.

One of the more notable land liquidations by Boise Payette Lumber Company occurred in the late 1930s and was spun into a positive public relations ploy by Shellworth and Moon. The two arranged for the company to gift the state 771 acres of timber land. Deeds to the parcels were presented at a dinner party in McCall as part of a multi-day tour of the region by the Idaho Cooperative Board of Forestry. At the event Harry presented Governor Bottolfsen a deed to 117 acres of land near Smiths Ferry and Moon presented C. Van Clark, the land board commissioner, with a deed to 654 acres of forested land on the north and east side of Payette Lake.[144] While the *Idaho Statesman* newspaper reported it as a "gift," it is more likely there was some benefit to the lumber company that was not reported such as the exchange of state timber. However, several years before the 771-acre deal with the

---

143 Hidy et al, 548.

144 "State Given Forest Land: Co-operative Board on Tour Gets Timber on Lake Shore," *The Idaho Daily Statesman*, 20 July 1939.

state, Boise Payette carved out a little more than seventy-six acres centered on Paradise Point on the east side of Payette Lake, fronting nearly 8,000 feet of shoreline.

The property encompassed large sandy beaches and beautiful granite rock formations and some of the best swimming areas on the lake, within a short distance from a series of islands paralleling the shoreline. The largest and most southern of the islands was originally named Cougar Island, but to honor Harry's work in the area in 1915, the state renamed it "Shellworth Island."[145] The seventy-six acres was divided into four lots extending north to south. In the summer of 1935, the two southern lots were granted to the Protestant Episcopal Church for the use as a summer camp, which eventually became named Paradise Point Summer Camp.[146] Moon was a layman in the Episcopal Church and worked closely with the bishop so the church could acquire the land.[147] The following year the church built the first improvement at the property in the form

---

145 Tom Grote, "Payette Lake islands face identity crisis; old names to resurface," *The Star News*, 22 August 1984. Sometime between the naming of Shellworth Island in 1915 and 1948, the three islands north of Shellworth were also officially named. The northern most island was named "Rhea Island" for Frank Rhea, who was a dean, and later a bishop at St. Michael's Cathedral in Boise. The next island to the south was named "Mather Island" and the one closest to Shellworth was named "Hewitt Island." Hewitt may be linked to a family that lived in Boise and were members of the church. The Boise State University Special Collections houses the Episcopal Diocese of Idaho Records (MSS 091) and with the assistance of Head Archivist Dr. Cheryl Oestreicher the names were researched. As per Dr. Oestreicher's research Mather is most likely named for Charles Mather (1883-1966) who was also a member of the church and an engineer for the Boise Payette Lumber Company. Interestingly, both the Hewitt and Mather names were used by the Boise Payette Lumber Company as street names for a residential development in McCall.

146 Valley County Recorder's Office, Deed Book 17, page 430, Instrument Number 20410.

147 Hidy et al, 536.

of a meeting hall known as "Barnwell Hall."[148] Since then the camp has provided generations of children access to the waters of Payette Lake and the surrounding mountains. Three years later Boise Payette Lumber Company granted more acreage (Lot 3) to the camp, bringing the total grounds to just over fifty-acres and more than six-thousand feet of shoreline.[149] This left only the northernmost parcel (Lot 4), consisting of more than twenty-six acres. The parcel was purchased by Harry in 1944 for his private use.[150] The seventy-six acres divided up by Boise Payette combined with the adjacent lands remains as some of the most pristine and naturally intact segments of Payette Lake. These waters and rocky shoreline accentuated by a chain of granite islands dotted with ancient twisted and gnarled pines are so breathtaking they equal any of the country's most remote and unspoiled mountain lakes. Reasonably, if it were not for Harry and Jack Moon, this expanse of Payette Lake would look very different. In fact, this area remains as one of the more inaccessible reaches of the lake. At the time the Episcopal Church acquired the property, however, it was only accessible by boat, before the road around the lake was finished by the CCCs in the winter of 1938-39.[151]

---

148 The meeting hall was named in honor of Bishop Middleton S. Barnwell, the seventh bishop of the Episcopal Diocese of Idaho. Most notably, Barnwell was instrumental in the formation of Boise Junior College (Boise State University) in the early 1930s and served as the president from 1932 to 1934.

149 Valley County Recorder's Office, Deed Book 19, page 433, Instrument Number 24534.

150 Valley County Recorder's Office, Deed Book 24, page 39, Instrument Number 32659. This property along with the parcels comprised to make up the Paradise Point Church Camp was derived from land Harry purchased as land scrip from the Aztec Land and Cattle Company LTD. The latter scrip company withdrew the parcels from the public domain in May 1906 and was recorded with the Government Land Office as BLM Serial Number IDIDAA038266FD—Document Number 14359.

151 "Lake Highway to be Completed," *Payette Lakes Star*, 13 October 1938.

On the west side of Payette Lake, the lumber company also held expansive tracts along the shoreline in the vicinity of the outlet of the lake and extending down the river to the fish hatchery. Considering the proximity of these lands to the downtown area of McCall and the anticipated postwar tourism boom, the company valued these properties for future development. In need of cash for the company, Harry approached several developers in the area, such as backcountry friend and owner of Burgdorf Hot Springs, Jim Harris. Harris had previously subdivided several large tracts on the shores of Payette Lake, including the Harris Cove Subdivision on the east arm. For unknown reasons, Harris declined to purchase, at which point Boise Payette subdivided and developed the lands itself.[152] The first of the subdivisions was land formerly leased to the CCC program for the McCall camp located across the street from the SITPA headquarters. Following the disbanding of the camp in August 1941, Boise Payette Lumber Company, as part of the war effort, donated the use of the mothballed facilities to the Army Air Corps/Force for a military convalescent summer camp for men stationed at Boise's Gowen Field.[153] Realizing the value of the lakefront property, the old camp was later subdivided into ten residential parcels under the name South Shore Subdivision. The plat was approved by the county in September

---

152 Dr. Scott Harris. Personal Communication. 28 January 2020. Scott is the grandson of Jim Harris.

153 Harry C. Shellworth. Letter to Mr. C. Kenneth DeLand Asst. Production Manager Paramount Pictures, Inc. 17 May 1946. Harry C. Shellworth Collection MS-269, Idaho State Historical Society. This is one letter in a series of correspondence between Harry and DeLand as Paramount was considering using McCall and surrounding areas to shoot the movie *Unconquered*. DeLand inquired with Harry about using the camp and property for the housing of movie crews. The outdoor scenes for the movie were ultimately shot elsewhere. The film was released in 1947.

1944.[154] After the war the CCC buildings were dismantled and the lots marketed. One of the first parcels sold was at the extreme eastern end of the subdivision, which was purchased by Warren Brown, the son of Harry's longtime friend and lumber competitor Carl Brown.[155] Warren and his wife Jayne built one of the areas earliest and largest mid-century modern homes at the site.

The next section of land subdivided was located just west of the Lardo Bridge over the North Fork of the Payette River and extended west along the shore toward Warren Wagon Road. This property was locally referred to as "Shellworth Beach" or "Shellworth Park" and contained a premier sandy beach with expansive views to the east, looking straight into the section of the lake known as "the Narrows." The Boise Payette Lumber Company subdivided this parcel into eight lots in November 1945 under the name Shellworth Park Subdivision.[156] However, the entire development was purchased by a single entity for the development of the Shore Lodge hotel. Again, Harry's friend Carl Brown was the president of the company's board of directors. The lodge opened in the summer of 1948 and has persisted as a center of community and tourist activity ever since.[157]

The last large parcel to be subdivided extended from the east side of Lardo Bridge, mostly south of Lake Street (Highway 55), north of the river/Mather Road, and west of State and Cross streets. The subdivision, with more than fifty residential lots, was approved in May

---

154 Valley County Recorder's Office, South Shore Subdivision plat.

155 Valley County Recorder's Office, Deed Book 26, page 81, Instrument Number 36081.

156 Valley County Recorder's Office, Shellworth Park Subdivision plat.

157 For more information on the history of Shore Lodge see: Darcy Williamson and Marlee Wilcomb. *McCall's Historic Shore Lodge 1948-1989.* McCall, ID: The Meadow Cottage Industries, 2007.

1946 and platted as Brundage Subdivision.[158] Harry even kept a lot as an investment, which his son later sold. A month after the Brundage Subdivision was approved, Harry and Jack Moon arranged for Boise Payette Lumber Company to donate several combined lots across the outlet of the lake from Shellworth Park/Shore Lodge to the city of McCall for public access to the lake.[159] The sandy beach and park eventually became known as Rotary Park and continues as a popular year-round park in the city's Parks and Recreation Department.

158 Valley County Recorder's Office, Brundage Subdivision plat.

159 Valley County Recorder's Office, Instrument Number 36343.

PAYETTE LAKE LOOKING NORTH AT SHELLWORTH ISLAND,
PARADISE POINT, AND SHELLWORTH PROPERTY.
(Holm photograph)

HARRY AT A "GOLD LACE LOOKOUT"
NEARING THE END OF HIS CAREER.
(Johnson & Son/Central Idaho Historical Museum)

9

SITPA—A LASTING LEGACY

*Packer John Lookout from which at an elevation of more than
7,000 feet is afforded a view which of its kind is second to none
in the State. The circumference swings around a microcosm of
Idaho, with timber as dense as meadow grasses, with mines in the
whole domain east of the Payette River, with agriculture in the
valleys, with cattle and sheep in the grazing areas of the forest,
and with a natural playground lying unbroken clear around the
compass. Everything that Idaho offers is summarized here.*
—VARDIS FISHER
Idaho Guide (1937)

Harry did not fully retire from forestry work until early 1949, when he left his position at SITPA. This slight delay allowed for a transition with the new Boise Payette executives onto the SITPA board. The Association continued to build upon Harry's hard work and conservation efforts, adapting to the ever-changing demands of urban interface fire policy and the ever-increasing population into the fire-prone timberlands throughout Boise and Valley counties. The SITPA board slowly changed into the current structure with the elimination of Harry's position of secretary-treasurer. The largest landholder in the organization still retains a board of director position, as was true in the Shellworth-era, thus having vast power in steering policy. In the modified arrangement, the chief fire warden of the Association works directly for the president of the board, who subsequently gets direction from the other board members, representing the interests and desires of the broader membership.[160]

The Association also changed how members joined and how the fees were collected. Following a series of large fires in the neighborhood of Garden Valley in the summer of 1966, which nearly bankrupted the Association, it was decided to collect membership fees as a line item on tax assessments from property owners based on private timbered acres within each respective county. The fees collected were then remitted to the Association and serve as the foundation of the operating budget. At the same time, the membership and fee collection changed the Association's cooperation with other land agencies; it also restructured the protection area into a more concentrated region centered on private timberlands in the vicinities of Cascade and McCall. The southern area in the lower parts of the Payette River drainages was largely eliminated.[161]

In the end, the reorganization left several of Harry's Gold Lace Lookout sites obsolete, among them Packer John and East Mountain.

---

160 Bill Williams. SITPA Chief Fire Warden 1991–2003, Personal Communication. 3 March 2020.

161 Williams, Personal Communication.

A decade earlier the Association had already relinquished use of Shafer Butte to the US Forest Service.[162] As for Packer John and East Mountain, it conducted a study where the scene areas of each of the lookouts, along with the neighboring lookouts, were mapped for historical fire activity.[163] The study concluded the most fire-prone areas, linked with the private timberlands under its jurisdiction, could best be watched from the Tripod Peak Lookout located to the west and owned by the Forest Service. With this in mind, SITPA entered an agreement with the Boise National Forest to cooperatively fund and staff the Tripod Lookout, and disposed of East Mountain and Packer John. The Association recognized the historical significance of the structures but did not have the funding or resources to save them. The Packer John Lookout was last staffed in the summer of 1979. The following June it was pulled down with a bulldozer, piled and burned in late September. The East Mountain Lookout was staffed into the 1990s, until it was donated to the Central Idaho Historical Museum, which planned with grants and volunteer labor to restore it. However, it burned down in a lightning-caused wildland fire in 2002.[164] The foundations of both are still visible.

In the midst of the changes on the southern end of the Association's protection area, the northern portion also underwent changes, including the removal of the Brundage Mountain Gold Lace Lookout. In its case, the CCC-built rock foundation was saved and a very utilitarian

---

162 The lookout building constructed in 1927 was replaced by the US Forest Service in 1958. Portions of the original rock and concrete foundation were utilized for the new building.

163 In relation to fire lookouts the term "scene area" references the visible terrain that can be viewed from the site.

164 Ray Cooper. SITPA Assistant Fire Warden 1974–2008, Personal Communication. 3 April 2020.

square lookout building, constructed of concrete masonry blocks, was erected in 1982–83 as a replacement. It is still in service. Slightly below the ridge to the west of this lookout sits the original 1914 Brundage Mountain log cabin that was relocated by the CCC in preparation for the construction of the 20' x 20' structure. Ownership of this improvement was transferred from SITPA to the Central Idaho Historical Museum, along with East Mountain. It is the only remnant from SITPA's first phase of fire lookout improvements, and believed to be the only surviving log cabin built entirely of whitebark pine in Idaho. The whitebark pine construction is unique, since it is an uncommon tree species for use in log cabin construction. Whitebark pine is now, rare, owing to attacks by mountain pine bark beetles. The attacks are exacerbated by a warming climate. The Central Idaho Historical Museum extensively stabilized the structure in the summer of 2009 and continues annual maintenance.

With all of these changes, the last example of Harry's Gold Lace Lookouts is No Business and it, too, has been somewhat modified. The logs on the main level were replaced with pre-cut D-Logs in 1963. However, the upper cab portions of the building still feature the full dovetail corners and original windows. The interior also remains largely original, with the Shellworth-era finishes and furnishings.

Just as the Association's lookout facilities underwent significant changes after Harry's retirement, the two headquarters did as well. By the late 1980s the facilities were in need of extensive improvements, which weighed heavily on the finances of the organization. Moreover, community growth in Cascade and McCall caused the organization to think about centralizing each of the headquarters to better serve members and the public. The extensive campuses were also becoming antiquated as SITPA no longer needed housing and bunkhouses, so much as more warehouse space for the larger and broader fleet of firefighting equipment.

Both the land for the Smiths Ferry and McCall complexes were deeded to the state of Idaho by Boise Payette Lumber Company, but restrictions within the deeds limited the use of the properties, and once no longer used for such activities as wildland firefighting, full ownership returned to Boise Payette or the closest related entity, which had become Boise Cascade. In the early 1990s, Chief Fire Warden Bill Williams and Assistant Fire Warden Ray Cooper worked with Boise Cascade and the state of Idaho on the disposal of the Smiths Ferry headquarters. Recognizing the historic significance of the property, it was listed on the National Register of Historic Places.[165] The property then reverted to Boise Cascade, which kept a large portion that once functioned as a tree farm. The acreage adjacent to Highway 55 containing the historic buildings was auctioned. The highest bidder was a private party. In the exchange Boise Cascade donated land and funded a new facility in Cascade. Specifically designed for SITPA, it officially opened in 1997.

Concurrent with the negotiations over Smiths Ferry, the McCall facility was also listed on the National Register of Historic Places in 1990.[166] The Bob Kirk family (chief fire warden from 1971 to 1990) was the last warden family to occupy the building before moving into a private residence in the mid-1980s. The rest of the site was still in use, but in desperate need of major repairs. Kirk's successor,

---

165 Elizabeth A. Egleston. National Register of Historic Places Registration Form —#90000681. 2 May 1990.

166 Elizabeth A. Egleston. National Register of Historic Places Registration Form —#90000680. 2 May 1990.

Bill Williams, was privy to management decisions affecting the local area on behalf of the state and Boise Cascade, because each continued the long tradition started by Harry of having a member from each organization sit on the SITPA board—Herb Malany for Boise Cascade and Winston Wiggins for the State Department of Lands. By happenstance, the Idaho Department of Lands was entertaining the idea of building a new facility in McCall at the same time SITPA was also looking to move from the old downtown site. The groups worked together, with the state agreeing to allow SITPA to join in on a cooperative building effort if Boise Cascade agreed to deed the McCall site to the state of Idaho. Initially, the move left many in doubt as to what would become of the historically significant site. It was well recognized, aside from the historical value, to possess substantial real estate value. Rumors spread that there were numerous potential bidders who intended to develop it into high-end condos. The rumors rapidly faded when Governor Cecil Andrus personally stepped in and guaranteed the state of Idaho would do everything to preserve the historic buildings and open space in downtown McCall.

The state of Idaho then approached the city of McCall about a possible deal. Both entities worried about the potential cost of maintaining the site, but in the end the city of McCall agreed to accept the property with the buildings as a gift. Similar to Harry's original arrangement when the Boise Payette Lumber Company deeded the property to the state of Idaho for SITPA's use, there were strings attached. The stipulations this time stated that the city of McCall had to maintain the facility, provide cultural interpretation, have it accessible to the public, and in the event that they no longer wanted the site, it could not be sold or subdivided, but rather it would revert to the state.

With no money in the city's budget to maintain or provide cultural interpretation, a grassroots nonprofit quickly formed to provide the necessary interpretation and to raise money for maintenance, primarily with grants. The nonprofit group operates as the Central Idaho Historical Museum and is comprised of a very dedicated group of volunteers. Since the museum's inception, the group has renovated the interior of various buildings to house offices, exhibits, archives, and artifacts associated with the history of the site, the community of McCall, and the related environs in the surrounding West Central Mountains. The crown jewel of the site is the Statehouse, which serves as the main stand-alone exhibit. The interior of the building is relatively unchanged from when it was finished in the late 1930s, with only slight changes to the kitchen and basement. The building is still adorned with most of the original furnishings, wall hangings, and décor. Historical interpretation has been added to aid visitors. The exterior of the building is also largely original, with the exception of brown logs stained instead of the original natural color, and the original wood shingled roof is covered by standing-seam metal—both modifications made by Chester "Chet" Putnam, who lived in the house with his family while chief fire warden from 1966 to 1970.[167]

The museum is open to the public during the summer, and tours of the Statehouse are typically available, along with exhibits featuring local history. Harry's long-lasting legacy in the West Central Mountains is well-recognized through the preservation of the former McCall SITPA headquarters and interpretive exhibits at the

---

167 Art Robert's daughters, Jo Peterson and Pat Benninghoff, along with their families and friends have donated time, labor, expertise and money to many of the Statehouse's preservation projects in the effort to restore and preserve the Statehouse as it appeared in the 1930s and 1940s.

museum. Furthermore, the continued longevity and stewardship of SITPA persist as one of Harry's greatest lasting impacts on the central region of Idaho.

PACKER JOHN LOOKOUT JUNE 1980. *(Ray Cooper Collection)*

RAY COOPER REMOVED PACKER JOHN LOOKOUT, JUNE 1980.
(Ray Cooper Collection)

EAST MOUNTAIN LOOKOUT SHORTLY AFTER A NEARBY
LIGHTNING-CAUSED FIRE IN 2002 IGNITED IT. NOTICE
DRAGON SHAPE VISIBLE IN THE FLAMES.
(Ray Cooper Collection)

NO BUSINESS LOOKOUT, 1930S – THE ONLY
REMAINING "GOLD LACE LOOKOUT."
(Johnson & Son/SITPA Collection)

BRUNDAGE MOUNTAIN LOOKOUT CABIN BUILT
1914 STILL STANDING. *(Holm photograph)*

10

GRANDAD HARRY— FAMILY MAN

Below is the deep blue serenity of Payette Lake, and on all sides
is the delicate lucid green of its streams. Mountains adjacent
look like mounds of chalk, or like slabs of granite adorned with
golden furze and tiny subalpine mirrors. Ranges now swim into
vision, with backbones serrated in row on row, with forested
depressions and altitudes stretching to the farthest reach.
—VARDIS FISHER
Idaho Guide (1937)

Harry's legacies to Idaho are widely evident and some of them
endure because he instilled conservation values and land ethics
in his family, his son, and his grandchildren. Following the "Courtship
Shadows," he and Stella bought a modest house in Boise's East End
neighborhood at 1415 E. State Street. Here they welcomed the birth

of their only child Eugene "Gene" Whitney in April 1912. By 1928 the Shellworths moved to a larger house ten blocks to the east at 300 E. Bannock Street.[168]

The present family remembers Stella through stories. A common thread was her support and love of Harry and his larger-than-life personality. Having lived in Boise most of her life, she had a vast network of friends, and she was quite involved in community social activities. She was content to support Harry and tend to the domestic affairs. The Shellworths frequently left Boise to vacation in McCall and enjoy Payette Lake. With Harry as a father, Gene had no choice but to be an outdoorsman, in the summer of 1924 he tagged along on his first of many pack trips into the Idaho Primitive Area, along with several members of the Frederick Weyerhaeuser family.[169] And, although Stella stayed home, Gene was often invited on Harry's auto tours as well. After high school, Gene attended the US Naval Academy in Annapolis, Maryland, where he played two seasons of football before graduating in 1935. About the time the Shellworth's moved to their forever home on E. Bannock Street, Stella's mother, Bessie, became bedridden, and for five years Stella served as her caregiver—thus tethered to Boise more so than Harry. Bessie died in June 1932 and Stella began coping with her own health problems. Referring to these difficult times, Harry wrote to a friend, "Mrs. Shellworth's mother

168 The Shellworth home at 300 E. Bannock remained in the family until 2001 when it was sold and converted to a medical office (Ada County Recorder's Office).

169 This trip is also significant as per Harry's correspondence the Weyerhaeusers filmed portions of the adventure. The whereabouts of the films are not known, but if they are in existence these would be the oldest moving film footage of the Middle Fork of the Salmon River and related environs, before Henry Weidner's 1926 film by two years. The footage is referenced in a letter from Frederick Weyerhaeuser to Mr. H.C. Shellworth dated 19 August 1925 and located in the Harry C. Shellworth Collection MS-269, Idaho State Historical Society Archives.

died early this spring and the release from her long invalidism (five years) was a benefit to Stella in relief from anxiety and constant care of her Mother, and since [then] she has become resigned to the loss of her own health but shows promise of improvement."[170]

The Great Depression was followed by the war-weary years of the early 1940s. Following his graduation from Annapolis, Gene remained far from home and served in the US Navy throughout the war. Always patriotic, Harry, in his mid-sixties, held a position on the local advisory board of occupational deferments; it enforced the regulations of the Selective Service Law. He was also appointed by Idaho Governor Chase Clark to serve on the executive committee of the Idaho Civil Defense Program. In 1944 Stella was diagnosed with colon cancer and one year later suffered an unrelated stroke.[171] She was seven years younger than Harry and died on October 17, 1945, at age sixty-one, and was buried in the Morris Hill Cemetery in Boise.[172]

After the war, Gene returned to Boise, where with his wife, Martha Buckley started his own family. Gene somewhat followed in Harry's footsteps, working for a time in the lumber business. He also took an interest in politics, serving two terms as Boise mayor (1961-1966). In the early 1960s Gene and Martha moved into the 300 E. Bannock Street house and raised their three children: Sandra "Sandy," born in 1944; Robert "Rob," born in 1947; and Harry "Toby," born in 1950. To his grandkids, Harry was simply known as "Grandad." When

---

170 Harry C. Shellworth. Letter to Mr. J.O. Stewart. 28 October 1932. Harry C. Shellworth Collection MS-269, Idaho State Historical Society Archives.

171 Stella Whitney Shellworth, Certificate of Death —State of Idaho —State File No. 145666.

172 "Prominent Boisean Dies: Mrs. Shellworth Succumbs Wednesday; Final Rites Pend," *The Idaho Daily Statesman*, 18 October 1945.

Harry officially retired, *The Idaho Daily Statesman* printed an article chronicling his career and revealing his retirement plans, stating, "He [Harry] now plans to devote all his time to hunting and fishing and to 'chumming around with my grandchildren.'"[173] And spend time with his grandkids he did—it became his priority. Both Gene and Martha worked fulltime, and when the children were young and not in school, Grandad Harry took them on adventures. The kids idolized him. What they best remembered about him was his love of nature, the outdoors, traveling, and for Rob, fly-fishing.

From an early age, Rob enjoyed his Grandad's jovial personality. Harry was still very active well into his seventies and eighties, and Rob spent many days in the outdoors with him, walking the wild areas near Boise, as well as fishing throughout southern Idaho. Looking back Rob said, "By the time I was fishing with him we did not go to lakes. It was live water or nothing. As for hunting—he no longer hunted big game, but he still hunted ducks." Rob only went hunting with Harry once. Harry invited him to join some of his old cronies to hunt his favorite spot west of Boise near the town of Star. It was cold, wet, and miserable. From then on, it was fishing trips only, even though in retrospect he had a good time because he was with Grandad.

More than any other outdoor activity, Harry loved fishing. To cast a line he traveled widely throughout his life. Over the years he fished most of the rivers in Idaho and ventured into Montana on the waters of the Gallatin, Madison, Jefferson, and Big Hole rivers. In his heart he most revered the fishery of the Middle Fork of the Salmon

---

173 "Pioneer Gem State Lumberman Ends 45 Years' Active Service," *The Idaho Daily Statesman*, 24 March 1949.

River. On the Middle Fork he fished for everything from cutthroat to rainbow trout, and from chinook salmon and steelhead to dolly varden. For shorter fly-fishing trips, he liked Silver Creek north of Ketchum. In his younger years, for more of a scenic experience, he enjoyed the high mountain lakes of the Sawtooths. Recalling some of his secret fishing holes to a friend in 1938, he wrote, "The Middle Fork is my favorite stream, except that I like Silver Creek for strictly orthodox dry-fly and Silver Creek is an ideal weekend stream. The lake fishing in the Sawtooth Mountains, with a good guide, is the last word in piscatorial delight, but Sawtooth lake fishing, like all things beautiful, and feminine, is also damned temperamental, and local knowledge of best lakes and their favorable conditions is necessary. Different Sawtooth lakes are stocked...The Champion and Washington lakes have some real 'tackle busters.' July and August are my favorite months on the Salmon River, or say June 20th to September 15th, and Sawtooth lakes are best in late July and all of August."[174] Harry's infatuation with fishing was well-known among his friends and acquaintances. Many letters and gestures of appreciation throughout Harry's career were accompanied by some form of fishing paraphernalia, ranging from small items such as hand-tied flies to larger ones such as a new set of hip waders. Notorious for not throwing away even the most worn-out piece of equipment, Harry's collection occupied a good portion of his garage, with two or three of the same item. The prize pieces in the collection, bamboo fly rods and their reels, were handed down to Rob as treasured mementos of Granddad Harry.

---

174 Harry C. Shellworth. Letter to Mr. Lee J. Falk. 31 January 1938. Harry C. Shellworth Collection MS-269, Idaho State Historical Society Archives.

Of all the reminiscences about Harry, none compare to the times spent at Grandad's property on the shores of Payette Lake. The memories are so etched in the grandkids lives that Harry and the landscape became one. As mentioned earlier, Harry's later years with the Boise Payette Lumber Company were burdened with the task of liquidating the company's land assets. In the process of selling it off, Harry purchased, with Jack Moon's approval, the northernmost lot adjacent to the land distributed years earlier to the Episcopal Church camp. In November 1944, Harry and Stella became the proud owners of their piece of paradise on Payette Lake. [175] In keeping with Harry's larger-than-life persona, his lake-front lot encompassed 26.09 pristine acres. More typical of the era were buyers who considered themselves fortunate to own a half-acre or acre lot on the lake. The Shellworth's property was one of a kind: boasting more than thirteen-hundred feet of granite shoreline extending north of the church camp, south of Ping Creek, and south of Lemah Creek. Harry first envisioned building a cabin on the property but with Stella's health deteriorating and his advancing age, the land became their private camping oasis: secluded beaches, swimming coves, diving rocks, several level camp flats.

The chunk of land became the focal point for family activities and was modestly referred to by the Shellworths as "The Property." It was here on extended camping trips where days were spent walking with Harry. On these occasions he shared with his grandkids his passion for the outdoors and its natural wonders. Harry instilled an appreciation and respect for nature and taught them about flora and fauna. He had a profound passion for botany; he enjoyed teaching them plant

---

175 Valley County Recorder's Office, Deed Book 24, page 39, Instrument Number 34185.

identification. Summer wildflowers were the most popular. Under Harry's influence, Rob and Sandy became lifelong botanical enthusiasts. It was not uncommon while on nature walks or backpacking trips for the Shellworth clan to challenge one another or a friend with the common as well as the Latin name of a plant species.

Reflecting on Harry's influence in her life, Sandy wrote her Grandad in 1966, while at college, expressing her appreciation: "I feel a deep debt of gratitude for the many things you gave and showed me as a youngster. I'll never forget the heritage of the outdoor, etc. which you gave to us kids. Every time I go into the mountains or just outdoors, I feel a love for and an understanding of the wild, growing things that live there. I feel happiness and peacefulness in the mountains. Now as I study plants and animals in college, I remember the first plants that you helped me collect! The golden buttercups, the bluebells, etc. Also I remember all the many things you pointed out and explained to us; the caterpillar tents, magpie nests, and meadowlark calls. You made us aware of things in the out-of-doors—few people are given the privilege of seeing the details of life; most people live in a haze. I hope this awareness of nature also will carry over into my complex daily life as this awareness did in your life, which enabled you to take advantage of and do so much, and what's more, to remember it all. I feel honored to be one of your grandchildren. I am very proud of you...Most of all, Grandad, I just want to thank you for being our grandad."[176]

Besides identifying and collecting wildflowers, the Shellworths picked huckleberries; in mushroom season they hunted morels. The

---

176 Sandy Shellworth. Letter to Harry Shellworth. 10 November 1966. Shellworth Family Collection.

expanse of the property provided plentiful berry patches and prime morel soil. And no Shellworth vacation was complete without fishing. Their private retreat had one of the best fishing holes on the lake where Ping Creek cut through the southern end of the property before it emptied into the lake. The stream was one of the few that attracted the inland-spawning kokanee trout.

At the end of a long day filled with canoeing, hiking, and swimming, or merely soaking up the mountain atmosphere, the family gathered around a campfire to share a good meal and swap stories. At the southern end of the property there was a choice camp spot—a level bluff with an unsurpassed view of the lake and Brundage Mountain. Large, evenly-spaced ponderosa pines were perfect for stringing hammocks, and the site was also close to Ping Creek, providing drinking water. At the center of the site a large level area hosted a huge granite boulder. Near it the family set up the portable outdoor kitchen stored in a hand-built, green cabinet. The boulder served as a sitting rock, table, and for reflecting the campfire. Around the fire and boulder, Harry, patriarch of the family and king storyteller, wove wonderful tales of his life's adventures. So taken by his stories and zest for travel, Sandy and Rob as adults also became world travelers. After graduating from Boise High School, Sandy went on to become a world class alpine skier, racing in college at the University of Colorado, Boulder (CU), and then as a member of the US Ski Team. She competed in the 1968 Winter Olympics held in Grenoble, France. After her ski-racing career ended, she settled permanently in Colorado with a career in the ski equipment industry. She married Ernie Hildner and they have two children, Cynthia and Andrew. Throughout Sandy's life she traveled with her family and visited every continent except Antarctica, and most of the noteworthy outdoor destinations in the United States.

After working his way through dental school at the University of Washington, Rob longed for adventure and took a job in British Columbia, Canada, providing dental care for indigenous people in rural areas across the province. He then moved on to doing similar work in Micronesia, mainly on the island of Palau. His world travels did not stop there; however, he decided to return to the US and settled in Idaho, starting a rural dental practice in Cascade and McCall in the early 1980s. Here he and his first wife, Janet, raised two daughters, Natalie and Sarah. In Cascade, Rob built his own house at the end of a long ridge south of Cascade with beautiful vistas across much of the land Harry cared for through his decades of conservation efforts at SITPA and the Boise Payette Lumber Company. When it came time to frame the house, his younger brother, Toby, helped him. By the 1990s Rob moved his residence and practice to Boise, divorced, and then married Jackie, and made Valley County his second home.

In spite everyone going in their own direction, "The Property" on the shores of Payette Lake persisted as a focal point in all of their lives, anchoring them together for family reunions and major events such as weddings. Gene, like his father, dreamed of building a cabin on the acreage at the family's favorite camping site. Like Harry's, the cabin never evolved beyond hand-drawn sketches. During the lifetime of both men, the extraordinary acreage was managed for its natural aesthetics, and timber-management consisted of occasional selective logging carried out to meet the requirements for county timber exemptions. The obvious tax advantages were one of the many benefits earned from management, but activities were a continuation of the conservation principles inspired by Harry. By the early 1990s, Gene and Martha were well into their retirement years and decided to sell eighteen acres of the northern portion of the property. The family kept seven-plus acres with the cherished family camping spot. Gene died in 1997 and Martha in 2005. Toby died in 2009, and Rob and Sandy, along with their families, continued to enjoy the property until they made the difficult decision, based on their own health, to sell the last seven acres in 2016. Sandy was diagnosed with cancer in September 2018 and passed away four months later.

Because of the Shellworths, the property still carries the conservation legacy so important to Harry, because each sale placed deed restrictions on the properties to prevent commercial development, and limited the number of allowable buildings. Compared to other areas of the lake, this stretch of land will be defined by the natural and wild landscape, forever rather than tiers of densely-stacked houses with owners eager for a slice of lake access.

SHELLWORTHS ON A FAMILY PICNIC AND FISHING TRIP, SOUTH FORK PAYETTE RIVER 1949. HARRY WITH GRANDKIDS, SANDY AND ROB, AND DAUGHTER-IN-LAW MARTHA "MARTY." (*Shellworth Family Collection*)

HARRY, SON GENE, AND WIFE STELLA IN 1935
AT GENE'S GRADUATION FROM THE US NAVAL
ACADEMY IN ANNAPOLIS, MARYLAND.
(Shellworth Family Collection)

11

HARRY THE REFLECTIVE

Boise offers a small playground in Julia Davis Park, with an
art museum, picnic grounds, boating, and tennis courts...
But Boise is more a center of a playground in itself, and it is
the side trips from there that offer the most in recreation.
—VARDIS FISHER
Idaho Guide (1937)

To no one's surprise Harry did everything but slow down in retirement. During the years before and after his eightieth birthday he continued making substantial life changes. To start with, he moved out of his longtime house on E. Bannock Street into the newly built, upscale, swanky Parkveiw Apartment complex on Crescent Rim Drive west of the Boise train depot. Situated on a natural bench above the city, his second-floor unit, walled with glass on the north elevation, along with a covered balcony, had panoramic views of the city he had called home for nearly seventy years. Overlooking Ann Morrison

Park and the tree-lined Boise River, his windows were filled by the seasonal colors of the Boise foothills and the outline of Shafer Butte— once home to one of his Gold Lace Lookouts. Considered deluxe for the time, the complex included a swimming pool and common areas adjacent to the city parks, and the location was within walking distance of places of upmost importance to Harry, such as the Arid Club and other downtown hangouts. If moving out of his house of thirty-some years was not enough, he remarried for a third time at eighty-two to Hazel Miriam Morrow. They were married in October 1959 at St. Michael's Episcopal Cathedral. At seventy-four, it was Hazel's first marriage, having pursued a lengthy and successful career as a nurse. Hazel was well-liked and affectionately called "Aunt Hazel" by Harry's grandkids. The title of "aunt" likely stemmed from the complicated family connection of Hazel's brother (McKeen) having been married to Stella Shellworth's sister (Helen). For most of the mid-to late-1960s Harry spent several winter months a year in La Paz, Mexico, on the Baja Peninsula, where he and Hazel enjoyed the mild climate and, of course, Harry ocean-fished.

Even though he dedicated more time to his family and leisure activities in retirement, he could not completely step away from his passion for conservation, preservation, and the accomplishments of a nearly fifty-year career. The Forestry Associations of Idaho nominated Harry as the Dean of Idaho Forestry in 1956. He was honored in McCall at a formal celebration. The certificate noted, "His [Harry] efforts helped initiate America's system of cooperative forest protection. In 1929 his timber protective association report first publicly voiced a nationwide slogan with 'Keep Idaho Green!' His pen was ready and used in establishing the 'Idaho Idea' as Idaho's forestry code and his wise counsel and guidance continues to maintain and advance the 'Idaho Idea' through the years."[177] Then in 1963 he was honored by *The Idaho Statesman* as a Distinguished Citizen. Such recognition even humbled the man who often attributed the success of his career to his careful behind the scenes work instead of the man being out front vying for recognition. Just as Harry had gained a reputation in the 1920s and 1930s as the definitive source on subjects such as the Idaho Primitive Area, his accumulation of knowledge and experiences connected with the events and development of Idaho forestry and the preservation of wildlands again made him a sought after person for interviews. Between 1955 and his death in 1973, Harry was interviewed by a number of emerging and established, American historians on subjects ranging from forestry to politics.

In the summer of 1955, historian Ralph W. Hidy, who specialized in business history, traveled to Boise to interview Harry. Hidy, a professor at New York University, was in the process of co-authoring a book about the Weyerhaeuser Company. The lengthy and in-depth conversation between the two men produced a ninety-page transcript, *The Reminiscences of H.C. Shellworth*. Two years after meeting with Harry, Hidy transferred to his alma mater, Harvard University, as a professor. There the book was finished with Frank Ernest Hill and Allan Nevins and published in 1963 as *Timber and Men: The Weyerhaeuser Story*. The exhaustive, seven-hundred-plus page book included facets of the company's Idaho operations, and for those details on the events south of the main Salmon River, Harry was credited.

---

177 Certificate from The Forestry Associations of Idaho archived in the Harry C. Shellworth Collection MS-269, Idaho State Historical Society Archives.

Hidy's interview was followed by another comprehensive one conducted by Elwood R. Maunder, the executive director of the Forest History Society. Maunder, at Shellworth's request, met with him while he was living in La Paz for a few months. Each day for a week, Maunder and Shellworth rendezvoused at the Los Cocos Hotel, where Maunder collected Harry's autobiography for the Forest History Society archives. The final interview was done by Michael P. Malone, then a doctoral candidate in American history at Washington State University, who was writing his doctoral dissertation on the late Governor C. Ben Ross. Malone's interests mainly pertained to Harry's relationship with Ross and the related New Deal efforts in Idaho. Harry and Malone did not exactly hit it off. Malone arrived at Harry's home without a tape recorder or a stenographer, which Harry felt was rude and unprofessional. Of all Harry's retained correspondence, his aggravation with Malone is among the only negative examples of his interactions with people. Voicing his irritation, he wrote a series of letters to Maunder venting, "Malone had his young wife with him, (acting as a stenographer), and his District Attorney's manner of repeating his questions with slight difference in phrasing; as if he was trying to confirm his own image of Gov. Ross rather annoyed me." Reiterating his sentiments toward the transcript of the Malone interview he continued, "I am sure you will have noticed the repetitions, questioning and 'District Attorney' manner of this young Pissant Malone. I could see that he was more interested in showing his bride (of 2 days) what a smart guy he was."[178] Regardless of Harry's distaste for Malone, his dissertation forms a worthy biography of

---

178 Harry C. Shellworth. Letter to E. R. Maunder. 27 August 1966. Shellworth Family Collection.

Ross, published by the University of Washington Press in 1970 as *C. Ben Ross and the New Deal in Idaho*. Harry was recognized as a contributor.[179]

Reading between the lines of Harry's correspondence regarding the three significant interviews, it is evident he was angling for either Hidy or Maunder to write his biography. In a letter to Maunder, he wrote, "I am very much in hopes of another session with you, as I am sure the SKY BOSS has started the 'count down' on me and I have a world of notes of my experiences that I am sure are valuable to history, on the basis of the wide range of experiences I lived thru..."[180] In fact, as the transcripts of the interviews were finalized after Harry's edits, he made dozens of copies and sent them to influential friends in an effort to generate interest in a biography. With the Hidy transcript in hand, he even reached out to his old literary friends—Vardis Fisher and Stewart Holbrook—testing whether his biography interested them. Both returned thoughtful letters, encouraging Harry to instead write an autobiography. From Hagerman, Idaho, Fisher wrote, "I found your reminiscences interesting but don't know if I am a fair judge, since I'm disposed in your favor. I'd think you could expand them to book size, for you must be as full of interesting anecdotes as a fruit cake with goodies."[181] Holbrook from Portland, Oregon, responded with a one-page letter observing, "Many of your references

---

179 Dr. Michael P. Malone went on to be a respected historian of the American West. His area of expertise was the history of Montana on which he published several noteworthy books. Malone ended his career as the 10th president of Montana State University in Bozeman. He died in 1995 at the age of 59 from heart complications.

180 Harry C. Shellworth. Letter to E. R. Maunder. 27 August 1966. Shellworth Family Collection.

181 Vardis Fisher. Letter to Harry Shellworth. 7 July 1958. The letter is presented in the front portion of a copy of Harry C. Shellworth, interview by Ralph W. Hidy, 1955, *The Reminiscences of H.C. Shellworth*, Oral History Research Office Weyerhaeuser Project, Forest History Society.

are of course cryptic—only teasers. They demand expansion if you decide to write a formal book. In any case, your direct approach to most of the subjects is refreshing. Should you go ahead with the book idea, I here and now want to place my order for a copy. I'm certain it will be almost as entertaining as spending an evening in your company ..."[182]

The interviews and sharing the transcripts with old and new friends delighted Harry. It stirred up good memories and he took the words of praise from people such as Fisher and Holbrook to heart. In August 1966, Hazel died, leaving Harry a widower for a third time. Before her death and in the subsequent years, he spent his free time revisiting the transcripts and reviewed his memorabilia boxes with files of old annual reports, decades of correspondence, photographs, and news clippings. Harry carefully went through every item, adding notes and labels as he saw fit. No doubt as he reminisced about the wonderful events of his life, he stared out his picture window and thought of all the trips to Shafer Butte, the park he dreamed of on the crest of the Boise Front, the hundreds of miles of incredible mountains he intimately knew and explored so many times, the countless adventures in the woods, and most of all the genuine people and relationships he treasured. Then at his feet, between the outlined hills and his veranda, was the city he grew up in and watched mature. In these surroundings, came the realization that no one was going to write his life story unless he put pen to paper. He concentrated on his early years in the transport service, the military, and travels. The

---

182 Stewart H. Holbrook. Letter to Harry Shellworth. 9 November 1957. The letter is presented in the front portion of a copy of Harry C. Shellworth, interview by Ralph W. Hidy, 1955, *The Reminiscences of H.C. Shellworth*, Oral History Research Office Weyerhaeuser Project, Forest History Society.

stories are succinct, anecdotal, characteristically have a punch line and are personified by his vocabulary, language and witty humor. He completed nearly a dozen of the stories. Proud of his work, he again sent them off to friends and family as early samples of more to come. Unfortunately, he did not complete more of them.

Harry died of natural causes on September 14, 1973, at the age of ninety-six. In the following weeks, regional and local newspapers ran numerous articles recounting his fascinating life and accomplishments—many pointing out his generosity and contributions to Idaho. One article published in *The Idaho Statesman* as an opinion piece by Bill Onweiler, a shirttail relative of the Shellworths, said it all with its headline: "The Most Unforgettable Man I Ever Met." Harry is buried alongside Stella in the Morris Hill Cemetery on the Boise Bench. Regarding Harry's funeral service, Onweiler observed in his newspaper tribute, "As I looked at Uncle Harry's casket I thought, 'How I envy this man who had truly run his cup over. Now Uncle Harry knows the final answer to the puzzle of existence.'"[183] Throughout Harry's life he seemed to find himself somehow involved with big events, and when people asked him about them, he quoted a Hindu-fortune teller in Rangoon, Burma, who had told him in December 1900, "You [Harry Shellworth] will be where things happen."[184] In light of his remarkable life one might more accurately say, "You, Harry Shellworth, made things happen."

---

183 Bill Onweiler. "The Most Unforgettable Man I Ever Met." *The Idaho Statesman.* 23 September 1973.

184 Harry C. Shellworth. Letter to E. R. Maunder. 27 August 1966. Shellworth Family Collection.

HARRY IN 1950S RELAXED, BUT NEVER FULLY RETIRED.
(Shellworth Family Collection)

POSTSCRIPT AND ACKNOWLEDGMENTS

While tilling under my vegetable garden for winter on a bright, beautiful October afternoon, my telephone rang. On the other end was Norm Zachary, an acquaintance I've known for years as people do in small communities. After catching up, he inquired about my recent history undertakings. Following a lengthy description of an ongoing and far from finished multi-year book project, there was a long pause, and then Norm's friendly voice broke in with, "Well that sounds fascinating." Another long pause, then he began explaining that he had a writing project for me. I quickly blurted "No," explaining that I already worked multiple jobs, have two young children, and a career-driven spouse. My spare time was limited. As a family man himself, he certainly understood. He continued, however, "Well, just let me explain the situation as I think you'll be interested. If nothing else I think you can provide some guidance." The story unfolded.

Norm, a lifelong friend of Rob Shellworth since their ski racing days as kids, informed me that Rob had recently been diagnosed with Alzheimer's disease. My heart sank. I knew Rob as well as I knew Norm—someone I had met a few times and always had good conversations with about shared interests: the outdoors, McCall, the Idaho backcountry, and of course his grandad.

My association with Rob stemmed from two previously published books on subjects tied to Harry—fire lookouts on the Payette National Forest, and the history of backcountry aviation in central Idaho. In the beginning, my parents provided the introduction—my mother knew Rob while growing up in Boise, and my father from a career in rural healthcare administration (when Rob practiced dentistry in Valley County). After our original meeting, Rob was always a great supporter of my history projects, sharing what he could about his grandad as they concerned my topics. At our meetings in Rob's home office, looking out on a stunning garden with views of downtown Boise, he discussed his longtime goal of writing his grandad's biography. Each time the subject arose he pointed to a low shelf with glass doors lined with neatly stacked vintage cardboard paper boxes containing Harry's papers. Each box was carefully labeled with catchy titles describing the contents. To a historian there is nothing more anticipated than unearthing primary documents or original historic photographs never used before, archived, published, or citied in scholarly work. The thought of what could be in the boxes tantalized me for years. While Rob was always forthcoming with information, it was unspoken that the contents of the boxes were off limits, because they were the foundation for the biography he planned to write someday.

By this point in the telephone conversation with Norm, I was leaning on my shovel, staring at the ends of my garden fence built around four-foot in diameter iron hay rake, wheels salvaged from a Chamberlain Basin homestead and given to me. I thought how ironic to be gazing at these wheels and discussing Harry Shellworth, for they had come from one of his favorite places. Norm jerked me out of my reverie when he said that the family would allow me to go through all of Harry's papers and memorabilia. Including access to the intriguing boxes kept in Rob's office. Norm emphasized time was of the essence because Rob's Alzheimer's had not completely arrested his long-term memory, but his was a disquieting prognosis. Rob's sister, Sandy, died of cancer earlier in the year and he was the last one of the immediate family to have firsthand memories of Grandad Harry. As a close friend, Norm was attempting to help Rob and his family put their affairs in order, and recounting the history of the family patriarch was one of their goals.

Norm organized a casual meeting at Rob's house for me to visit with the Shellworths about some options for Harry's papers, as well as to look through the collection. Rob's wife Jackie put together an excellent lunch and I had the privilege of visiting with them all in person, including Rob's niece Cynthia Hildner, Sandy's oldest child. We discussed a number of options as to university libraries and archives where the collection might most appropriately be curated for the future. By the end of the several-hour visit, I was reminded how much Harry Shellworth fascinated me. As the social gathering wound down I held to my decision of not wanting to write a book, citing my skills were inadequate to write a comprehensive biography, as well as my lack of time. However, I felt an overwhelming obligation to at least help keep Harry's name alive, and pitched the idea of writing an article to be submitted to a local or regional magazine. Cynthia and Jackie were immensely helpful in igniting the process by labeling the papers and boxes I was most interested in, and making copies for me.

For a month, I spent evenings reading through the papers that Harry had retained. I re-read the extensive interviews conducted with Harry by Hidy, Maunder, and Malone, which I had purchased more than ten years earlier from the Forest History Society. I also reviewed a large stack of photocopies I had made years ago of his correspondence donated to the Idaho State Historical Society Archives. Using the narrative of Harry's contributions to Idaho, the article began to take shape, but I kept discovering one more interesting fact or story, and before I knew it the project exceeded a typical 3,500-word article. I then convinced myself a two-part article at twice the length would suffice. It, too, failed to fit. In the process of writing and collecting, I began piecing pages together. Comparing the papers retained by the Shellworth family with those from the Idaho State Historical Society, along with letters from Harry on the subjects in his files, I noticed duplications. I then revisited the Idaho State Historical Society and pulled all the items that Harry had donated in 1966. I discovered that Harry had in fact donated most of his correspondence and work-related papers to the Historical Society, but for whatever reasons, some of them were retained, in a mix of originals and copies. I also realized that in both collections Harry had annotated, when he thought appropriate, various papers and documents. This provided me with not only the primary document with his thoughts at the time, but also his retrospective insights on the matters forty and fifty years later—truly fascinating.

Inundated in the life of Harry Shellworth, I teetered between scrapping most of what I'd written for the article, and beginning all over with a book. For weeks I vacillated. While undecided, I noticed things in my everyday environment that existed because of

Shellworth's influence. These ranged from open space as parks, to stepping out any door of my house and seeing a mountain where one of his Gold Lace Lookouts stood (or once stood), or the trail near my house where I take my children walking and skiing daily that was once the railroad built to move Boise Payette Lumber Company logs to Emmett. His impact on the central region of Idaho was overwhelming, and the more I thought about it, the more dumbfounded I was to think that so little recognition had been given him. I thought of my ten years on the board of the Central Idaho Historical Museum, caring for the old SITPA campus, and one of the best days of my life was at his cherished Statehouse, because it was where my wife and I held our wedding reception. Then I thought of all the times I've retraced and crisscrossed Harry's tracks in the backcountry, flying, hiking, and fishing his beloved haunts on the Middle Fork of the Salmon River, Big Creek, and Chamberlain Basin—his foresight in setting aside one of the most peaceful and well-preserved stretches of wilderness left in the world was his monumental achievement. During these few weeks of debating about an article or a book, it was as if the spirit of Harry Shellworth was as persuasive as he was fifty years ago, working his political magic behind the scenes. I committed. Naturally, there are many ways to approach such a book: forestry, politics, conservation, preservation. I chose to focus on his major contributions to the state of Idaho, and on those areas of his life that have been neglected. Harry's involvement with the Idaho Primitive Area has often been explicated in books and scholarly articles. I chose to concentrate on information not yet addressed, and summarized those actions and events to which nothing new can be added.

Galvanized by the idea of a book, research intensified in an effort to round out Harry's overall life and explore how his achievements appear at present. To accomplish this, extensive primary and secondary sources were utilized. Frequent trips were made to the Valley County Courthouse to trace property deeds related to Boise Payette Lumber Company real estate. I also spent time tracking down the whereabouts of papers and archival collections separate from the personal papers he kept at the time of his retirement. Shellworth-related material in the form of photographs and correspondence exists in several other collections at the Idaho State Historical Society Archives, such as the CCC in Idaho Collection, the William Borah Collection, and the James H. Hawley Collection. Additionally, there are other collections with connection to Shellworth held at the University of Idaho Library's Special Collections, such as the David Lewis Papers and the Jewett Collection. Shellworth correspondence related to the formation of the Idaho Primitive Area is also on file at the US Forest Service Intermountain Region Office in Ogden, Utah. When Harry left his position with SITPA, he took only those items of personal interest. Many copies of his forestry publications, booklets, annual reports, and other more generic administrative materials were left behind. Most of this material has been preserved by the Central Idaho Historical Museum, while some of it can also be found on file at the SITPA headquarters in McCall.

Historians with overlapping interests were also consulted, as well as people with specific knowledge about subjects directly or indirectly related to Harry. For historic generalities on logging and timber in the West, Dr. Adam Sowards, an environmental history professor at the University of Idaho, made invaluable contributions as a sounding board and provided directions for reliable references. In the same arena of Harry's life, but on a more local level, John Kwader and Barbara Nokes Kwader also provided significant suggestions and contacts. John spent a career working as a professional forester for Boise Cascade. He and his wife Barbara have measureless local knowledge of forestry in Valley County and manage the nearly 2,000-acre Herald Nokes Family Experimental Forest in conjunction with the University of Idaho's College of Natural Resources. Much of the land comprising the experimental forest was originally acquired by Harry for the Boise Payette Lumber Company, logged, and then sold by Harry directly to the Nokes family. To sort out the complexities of Harry's involvement with the Civilian Conservation Corps, historians Dr. Pat Hart and Ivar Nelson shared their extensive personal knowledge on the subject, as well as years of their on-going research collected to build the complete "CCC in Idaho" digital archive at the University of Idaho Library. In an effort to counterbalance some of Harry's masterful storytelling with more exacting dates and facts, I relied on genealogical research conducted by friend Gayle Dixon and her mother Eleanor Dixon. Helping to bring Harry's character and demeanor into the text were Pat Benninghoff and Jo Peterson, the daughters of Art Roberts, who was the SITPA chief fire warden from 1944 to 1966. Their written and verbally shared recollections of Harry were delightful. Good friend, Cort Conley, fellow Salmon Riverophile and retired director of literary services for the Idaho Commission on the Arts, provided immeasurable assistance in sorting out Harry's numerous literary connections and historical ties to the backcountry. Thank you to Bruce Reichert for penning the foreword. Moreover, the book would not be possible without Rob, Jackie, and Ernie Hilder, and Norm who entrusted me to tell some of Harry's story. Throughout the development of the project they were patient and put up with my continual questions.

Lastly, to my father, Richard Holm, Sr., who sparked my interest in history when I was "knee high to a grasshopper." From a young age, I tuned into stories of the old days of McCall and the surrounding mountains told by family. There was something perplexing and intriguing about experiencing the exact same space and environment enjoyed by my parents, grandparents and great grandparents. From those stories I came to know old-time names in the area such as Blackwell, Stringer, Luck, Harris, Brown, Boydston, Rowland, and many others. Shellworth was also among those names, which in my young mind I associated with the island on the lake and the big rocks south of North Beach. And no history project of mine would ever be complete or possible without the continual support of my family—especially from my wife, Amy. Others who contributed enormously to this body of work include: Jim and Holly Akenson, Ed Allen, Tor Andersen, Al Becker, Kurt Becker, Bill Brown, Eve Brassey Chandler, Dr. Teresa Cohn, Dave Cook, Ray Cooper, Kathy Deinhardt Hill, Earl Dodds, Mike Dorris, Max Eiden, Ann Lloyd Edwards, Frank Eld, Jeff Fereday, Scott Findlay, Peter Gag, Matt and Ellen Ganz, Margaret Gorrissen, Nancy Greaves, Julie Grove, Dr. Scott Harris, Bernice Heikkila Hendrix, Shannon Henggeler, Ellen Holm, Kay Hummel, Carolyn Johnson, Rick Just, Tom Kerr, Larry Kingsbury, Paul Klasner, Ray Kresek, Allan Maki, John McCarthy, Sandy McRae, Peter Morrill, Dr. Cheryl Oestreicher, Stefani Patten, Amy Pemberton, Walt Sledzieski, Walt Smith, Jack Trueblood, Catherine Wardwell, Gary Weber, Marlee Wilcomb, Bill Williams, Kurt Wolf, Dr. Mark Wolfenden, Mark Woods, Tim Woodward, and Morgan Zedalis.

Selected Bibliography

Austin, Judith. "CCC in Idaho." *Idaho Yesterdays 27* (Fall 1983), 13-17.

Baird, Dennis, and Lynn Baird. "A Campfire Vision: Establishing the Idaho Primitive Area." *Journal of the West* (July 1987).

Bold, Christine. *WPA Guides: Mapping America.* Jackson, MS: University Press of Mississippi, 1999.

Brown, Nelson C. Letter to Harry C. Shellworth. 29 May 1937. Shellworth Family Collection.

Brown, Warren Harrington. *It's Fun to Remember: A King's Pine Autobiography.* Boise, ID: Self-published, 1999.

Borah, William E. Letter to Harry C. Shellworth. 13 September 1927. Shellworth Family Collection.

Carrey, Johnny, and Cort Conley. *River of No Return.* Cambridge, ID: Backeddy Books, 1978.

Carrey, Johnny, and Cort Conley. *The Middle Fork: A Guide.* Cambridge, ID: Backeddy Books, 1992.

CCC in Idaho Collection MS-683. Idaho State Historical Society Archives.

Chatterton, Wayne. *Vardis Fisher: The Frontier and Regional Works.* Western Writers Series—Boise State College, 1972.

Clark, D. Worth. "Idaho Made the Desert Bloom." *The National Geographic Magazine.* June 1944.

Cooper, Ray. SITPA Assistant Fire Warden 1974—2008. Personal Communication. 3 April 2020.

Doig, Ivan. "The Baedeker of Idaho." *Pacific Search: Northwest Nature and Life.* June 1978, 21-23.

Eagan, Harry. Burial File, National Archives. RG92, Stack Area 3/70, Row 65, Compartment 11, Shelf 7, Box 1458.

Egleston, Elizabeth A. National Register of Historic Places Registration Form —#90000680 (McCall SITPA Site). 2 May 1990.

Egleston, Elizabeth A. National Register of Historic Places Registration Form —#90000681 (Smiths Ferry SITPA Site). 2 May 1990.

Eld, Frank W. *Finnish Log Construction—The Art: The Story of Finnish Log Construction in America.* Donnelly, ID, F.W. Eld, 2013.

Fisher, Vardis. *Idaho: A Guide in Word and Picture.* Caldwell, ID: The Caxton Printers, Ltd, 1937.

Fisher, Vardis. Letter to Harry Shellworth. 7 July 1958. Shellworth Family Collection.

Fuller, Margaret, Doug Fuller, and Jerry Painter. *Ski the Great Potato: Idaho Ski Areas Past and Present.* Weiser, ID: Trail Guide Books, 2013.

Girard, Franklin. *Chateau de Bois: Idaho Cooperative Board of Forestry.* (May 1940). Holm Collection.

Gorrissen, Margaret. Personal Communication. 8 May 2020.

Grote, Tom. "Payette Lake islands face identity crisis; old names to resurface." *The Star News.* 22 August 1984.

Harris, Dr. Scott. Personal Communication. 28 January 2020.

Hidy, Ralph W. *The Reminiscences of H.C. Shellworth* (interview with Harry C. Shellworth). 1955 Oral History Research Office Weyerhaeuser Project, Forest History Society.

Hidy, Ralph W., Frank Ernest Hill, and Allan Nevins, *Timber and Men: The Weyerhaeuser Story*. New York, NY: The Macmillan Company, 1963.

Holbrook, Stewart H. *Burning an Empire: The Story of American Forest Fires*. New York, NY: The Macmillan Company, 1943.

Holbrook, Stewart H. Letter to Harry Shellworth. 9 November 1957. Shellworth Family Collection.

Holland, Wendolyn. *Sun Valley: An Extraordinary History*. Nampa, ID: The Idaho Press, 1998.

Holm, Richard H., Jr. *Points of Prominence: Fire Lookouts of the Payette National Forest*. McCall, ID: Cold Mountain Press, 2009.

Holm, Richard H., Jr. *Bound for the Backcountry: A History of Idaho's Remote Airstrips*. McCall, ID: Cold Mountain Press, 2013.

Johnson, Carolyn. Personal Communication. 10 February 2020.

Jordan, Grace. *The King's Pines of Idaho: A Story of the Browns of McCall*. Portland, OR: Binfords & Mort Publishers, 1961.

Just, Rick. Personal Communication. 10 February 2020.

Koch, Elers. *Forty Years A Forester: 1903-1943*. Missoula, MT: Mountain Press Publishing Company, 1998.

Kresek, Ray. *Fire Lookouts of the Northwest*. Spokane, WA: Historic Lookout Project, 1998.

Lehman, Eben. "Forgotten Characters from Forest History: 'The Guberif,'" *Peeling Back the Bark: Exploring the collection, acquisitions, and treasures of the Forest History Society*. January 2011.

Lewis, David. Letter to Col. W. C. Brown. 1 February 1925. W.C. Brown Collection, University of Colorado at Boulder Archives.

Lukas, J. Anthony. *Big Trouble: A Murder in a Small Western Town Sets Off a Struggle For the Soul of America.* New York, NY: Simon & Schuster, 1997.

Maki, Allan and Bernice Heikkila Hendrix. Personal Communication. 26 May 2020.

Malone, Michael P. Interview with Harry Shellworth. Forest History Society, 1964.

Malone, Michael P. *C. Ben Ross and the New Deal in Idaho.* Seattle, WA: University of Washington Press, 1970.

Maunder, Elwood R. *Transcript of Maunder-Shellworth Tapes—Version #1 Unedited.* Forest History Society, 1963. There are two transcript versions of the Maunder-Shellworth interviews. Based on conversations with Forest History Society archivists the transcripts were created from the same interview tapes conducted by Maunder in 1963. For clarification as to the source they are referenced as Version #1 and Version #2. Version #1 is lengthier, lacks edits, and includes information not included in the more refined version. Version #2 is more condensed and has been edited.

Maunder, Elwood R. *Transcript of Maunder-Shellworth Tapes—Version #2 Edited.* Forest History Society, 1963. There are two transcript versions of the Maunder-Shellworth interviews. Based on conversations with Forest History Society archivists the transcripts were created from the same interview tapes conducted by Maunder in 1963. For clarification as to the source they are referenced as Version #1 and Version #2. Version #1 is lengthier, lacks edits, and includes information not included in the more refined version. Version #2 is more condensed and has been edited.

McCormick, Anne O'Hare. *An American Epic in Sand and Flame.* SITPA, 1931. Holm Collection.

McCormick, Francis J. Letter to Mr. Harry C. Shellworth. 6 March 1933. Shellworth Family Collection.

McFarland, Ron, and Hugh Nichols (editors). *Norman Maclean: American Authors Series*. Lewiston, ID: Confluence Press, Inc., 1988.

McKenna, Marian C. *Borah*. Ann Arbor, MI: The University of Michigan Press, 1961.

Minshall, G. Wayne. *Cabin Creek Chronicle: The History of the Most Remote Ranch in America*. Inkom, ID: Streamside Scribe Press, 2014.

Morton-Keithley, Linda. National Register of Historic Places Registration Form —#94001451 (The Rocky Mountain Club). 9 December 1994.

Onweiler, Bill. "The Most Unforgettable Man I Ever Met." *The Idaho Statesman*. 23 September 1973.

Peek, Pat Cary. *Cougar Dave: Mountain Man of Idaho*. Bend, OR: Maverick Publications, 2004.

Peterson, Jo (Roberts). Letter to Richard Holm, Jr. 24 January 2020.

Reinikka, Merle A. *Finnish Settlers of Long Valley, Idaho*. (Portland, OR: Finnish American Historical Society of the West, 1990).

Rettig, E.C. Letter to Harry C. Shellworth. Land Agent Boise Payette Lumber Company. 30 December 1930. Harry C. Shellworth Collection MS-269, Idaho State Historical Society Archives.

Robison, Ken. *Defending Idaho's Natural Heritage*. Boise, ID: Self-published, 2014.

Rutledge, R.H. Letter to Mr. R. E. Shepherd. 26 June 1936. Harry C. Shellworth Collection MS-269, Idaho State Historical Society Archives.

Scribner, S.C. *Idaho Primitive Area Report*. USDA, Forest Service: 17 March 1931. Holm Collection.

Shellworth, Harry C.
- Annotated note on a newspaper clipping regarding the Battle of Manila, found in the newspaper clipping file within the Harry C. Shellworth Collection MS-269, Idaho State Historical Society Archives.
- *Annual Report: Southern Idaho Timber Protective Association 1927*. SITPA, 1927. Harry C. Shellworth Collection MS-269, Idaho State Historical Society Archives.
- *Annual Report: Southern Idaho Timber Protective Association 1929*. SITPA, 1929. On file at the SITPA office in McCall, ID.
- Letter to Mr. J.O. Stewart. 4 December 1930. Harry C. Shellworth Collection MS-269, Idaho State Historical Society Archives.
- Letter to Mr. J.O. Stewart. 13 January 1931. Harry C. Shellworth Collection MS-269, Idaho State Historical Society Archives.
- *Annual Report: Southern Idaho Timber Protective Association 1931*. SITPA, 1931. Harry C. Shellworth Collection MS-269, Idaho State Historical Society Archives.
- Annotated note written in the margins of a letter from E.C. Rettig. 30 December 1931. Harry C. Shellworth Collection MS-269, Idaho State Historical Society Archives.
- Letter to Mr. J.O. Stewart. 28 October 1932. Harry C. Shellworth Collection MS-269, Idaho State Historical Society Archives.

- Report of Work by Southern Idaho Civilian Conservation Corps Camps to Governor C. Ben Ross. February 1934. Harry C. Shellworth Collection MS-269, Idaho State Historical Society Archives.
- Letter to Mr. R.E. Shepherd. 27 June 1936. Harry C. Shellworth Collection MS-269, Idaho State Historical Society Archives.
- Letter to Stanly A. Easton. 17 May 1937. Harry C. Shellworth Collection MS-269, Idaho State Historical Society Archives.
- Letter to Mr. Lee J. Falk. 31 January 1938. Harry C. Shellworth Collection MS-269, Idaho State Historical Society Archives.
- Letter to Mr. C. Kenneth DeLand Asst. Production Manager Paramount Pictures, Inc. 17 May 1946. Harry C. Shellworth Collection MS-269, Idaho State Historical Society.
- *Courtship Shadows.* 1963. Shellworth Family Collection.
- Letter to E. R. Maunder. 27 August 1966. Shellworth Family Collection.
- *Travel-Log North Pacific Ocean (1893-1904).* March 1970. Shellworth Family Collection.

Shellworth, Sandy. Letter to Harry Shellworth. 10 November 1966. Shellworth Family Collection.

Swan, Kenneth D. *Splendid Was the Trail.* Missoula, MT: Mountain Press, 1968.

Taber, Ronald W. "Vardis Fisher and the 'Idaho Guide." *Pacific Northwest Quarterly* (April 1968), 68-76.

The Idaho Daily Statesman
- "The most brilliant social event of the week was the wedding of Miss Ida Himrod and Harry Shellworth," Boise Society Section, 18 September 1904.
- "Mrs. Ida Shellworth Dies At Hospital: Succumbs at St. Luke's From Peritonitis," 9 April 1905.
- "Report Lauds Forest Work: CCC Given Credit for Preventing Damaging Fires in Local Areas," 6 February 1934.
- "Gray Inspects Stanley Basin: President of Union Pacific party Interested in Resort Development," 11 July 1936.
- "*The Idaho Daily Statesman's* Monday Picture Page [featuring Packer John Lookout],"19 October 1936.
- "Fleeing Sheepherder Gives Name to New Idaho Lookout," 15 November 1936.
- "Movie Scouts Coming Today: Picture Officials to Study McCall Area as Film Site," 26 April 1938.
- "State Given Forest Land: Co-operative Board on Tour Gets Timber on Lake Shore," 20 July 1939.
- "Veteran Forest Lookout Ends Career," *The Idaho Daily Statesman*, 28 January 1940.
- "Nearby Boise Ridge Holds Rich Scenic Beauties," 14 October 1945.
- "Prominent Boisean Dies: Mrs. Shellworth Succumbs Wednesday; Final Rites Pend," 18 October 1945.
- "Pioneer Gem State Lumberman Ends 45 Years' Active Service," 24 March 1949.

Weyerhaeuser, Frederick. Letter to Mr. H.C. Shellworth. 19 August 1925. Harry C. Shellworth Collection MS-269, Idaho State Historical Society Archives.

Williams, Bill. Personal Communication. 3 March 2020.

Williams, Gerald W. *The Forest Service: Fighting for Public Lands.* Westport, CT: Greenwood Press, 2007.

Williamson, Darcy, and Marlee Wilcomb. *McCall's Historic Shore Lodge 1948-1989.* McCall, ID: The Meadow Cottage Industries, 2007.

Woodward, Tim. *Tiger on the Road: The Life of Vardis Fisher.* Caldwell, ID: Caxton Printers, 1989.

Wylie, Jerry. *Cultural Resource Inventory of the Warren Wagon Road Idaho and Valley Counties, Idaho, Payette National Forest.* McCall, ID: Payette National Forest, 1981.

Youngdahl, Kristi M. *The Arams of Idaho: Pioneers of Camas Prairie and Joseph Plains.* Moscow, ID: University of Idaho Press, 1995.

INDEX

A

B

Boise Basin, 8, 31, 48

Boise Bench, 169

Boise Cascade Corporation, 130, 143-144, 177

Boise County, 140

Boise Front, 115, 168

Boise High School, 3, 158

Boise Mountain Park, 49-50, 168

Boise National Forest, 141

Boise Payette & Manufacturing Company, 6-7

Boise Payette Lumber Company, iii, 7-9, 12, 23, 39, 48-49, 56, 58, 95, 110, 124 -135, 139, 143-144, 156, 159, 175-177

Boise Ridge, 46

Boise River, 8, 164

Borah, Cavanah, and Blake, 6

Borah, William, iii, 5, 42, 50, 84, 102-104, 110

Boston, Massachusetts, 4

Bottolfsen, Clarence A., 42, 130

Boulder White Clouds, 108

Boxer Rebellion, 4

Brooklyn, New York, 2

Brown, Bill, 178

Brown, Carl, 9, 56, 73, 120-122, 134

Brown, Jayne, 134

Brown, Nelson C., 80

Brown, W.C., 93, 95

Brown, Warren, 122, 134

Brundage Mountain Lookout, 25-26, 28-29, 32, 34, 55, 64, 66, 71-72, 141-142, 149, 158

Brundage Subdivision, 135

Buckley, Martha, 153

Bureau of Reclamation, 44

Burgdorf Hot Springs, 57, 133

Burning an Empire, 55, 115

C

C. Ben Ross and the New Deal in Idaho, 41, 167

Cabin Creek, 83

Caldwell, Idaho, 14

I

R

S

V

W

About the Author

The author—Holm is a fourth generation Idahoan who is a commercial pilot and outdoor enthusiasts with a fascination of Idaho history, especially topics related to the remote backcountry areas. He has written numerous pieces related to backcountry flying and fire lookouts. When not collecting information for the latest writing project, Holm resides in McCall with his wife Amy, their two children, and golden poodle.

AUTHOR—MIDDLE FORK OF THE SALMON RIVER—
FRANK CHURCH RIVER OF NO RETURN WILDERNESS.
(Holm Collection)

CPSIA information can be obtained
at www.ICGtesting.com
Printed in the USA
FSHW011956070821
83747FS

9 780578 856094